kNOT unDONE

Laura Schultz

LITTLE CREEK PRESS
AND BOOK DESIGN
Mineral Point, Wisconsin USA

Copyright © 2022 Laura Schultz

Little Creek Press®
A Division of Kristin Mitchell Design, Inc.
5341 Sunny Ridge Road
Mineral Point, Wisconsin 53565

Book Design and Project Coordination:
Little Creek Press and Book Design

First Printing
April 2022

All rights reserved

No part of this book may be used or reproduced
in any manner whatsoever without written
permission from the author.

Printed in the United States of America

For more information or to order books,
www.littlecreekpress.com

Library of Congress Control Number: 2022905682

ISBN-13: 978-1-955656-17-7

To contact Laura Schultz:
authorlauraschultz@gmail.com
@authorlauraschultz

For every individual who has stood at the edge of darkness, questioning whether today was the day.

CONTENTS

7 | PROLOGUE	67 | RESOLUTE	127 | RECONCILIATION
9 | JEALOUSY	70 | GOODBYE	129 | FOOLISH
12 | IRRITATION	73 | DISGUST	132 | COMMITMENT
16 | ENVIOUS	75 | TRAPPED	134 | DEFEAT
21 | INADEQUATE	79 | SHAME	138 | REFRESHED
24 | EUPHORIC	81 | HESITANT	141 | DEDICATION
28 | REELING	83 | STUNNED	144 | PEACE
32 | DISBELIEF	88 | CONFUSED	146 | INSPIRED
35 | DEVIOUS	90 | SELF-CONSCIOUS	150 | REFLECTION
38 | SATISFIED	93 | INEPT	153 | DETERMINED
41 | BITTER	97 | SHY	156 | HOPE
43 | RESENTMENT	100 | RESTLESS	159 | CONTENT
47 | DESOLATION	102 | MOTIVATED	162 | RUMINATE
48 | RELIEF	105 | INSECURE	165 | PROUD
51 | FEAR	109 | DEPENDENCE	168 | RENEWAL
55 | DESPAIR	113 | MISERY	170 | RESOURCES
59 | POTENTIAL	117 | OVERWHELMED	172 | ACKNOWLEDGMENTS
63 | WORTHLESS	121 | SHOCK	175 | ABOUT THE AUTHOR
65 | INTRIGUE	122 | CONTEMPT	

PROLOGUE

"All right. I'll call you later."

If only.

Words as such never spoken to me.

Ignored. Scratch that—unseen by any of my peers.

No one talks, waves, or even acknowledges my presence.

All I am is the locker space separating them from their friends.

What can I do to make them see me?

Flattery, belligerence, flat-out meanness?

Nothing works.

My absence is the only thing left to establish my existence.

Even that fails.

"That girl? Oh, she was the girl who always ... well, you know."

JEALOUSY

"Did you see what Madison wore to Kyle's party on Friday night?"

"She must think Kyle is on the market again after the showdown between him and Annika last week."

"She better get in line. Every girl in this school would want to sign up for that prize if they actually broke up."

Yes! That was exactly the piece of gossip I needed to pick me up after a bad morning. I was checking my notifications from Facebook and Instagram during lunch hour in the mezzanine when I overheard the whispers of the nearby group of girls. Social media was my saving grace to stay informed about most of the stuff happening at school, but the juiciest bits of gossip were always still revealed in person.

I knew every detail of every rumor—legitimate or otherwise—within the walls of Glenmore High. I could remember everyone's name, relationship status, who went out with whom and for how long, and everyone's history they wish was forgotten, but ironically, nobody even knew my name. When I went to the office, I had to show my identification card every single time because no one ever remembered I was a student there. It was as if my record was nowhere and had never been anywhere. The secretaries gave me those looks usually reserved for the teenagers loitering on the street corner who caused them to hold onto their purse a little tighter as they walked past.

You're probably thinking, "Oh, poor teenage girl. Couldn't make it with the normal girls in high school." And you're right; I couldn't make it in their world. I had never been able to. It started in first grade when we needed to pair up with another student, and there was an odd number, so I did my activity with the teacher. I remember she had to leave me alone to deal with a troublemaker, so I was left to watch everyone else have fun. From that day forward, I had been the odd one out. The one who didn't get to play kickball because it would make uneven teams, the one who sat alone in the bus seat for field trips, the one who stood awkwardly at the side of the gym at school assemblies, the one always left out of everything. I never got invited to the coveted sleepovers and, to this day, have never spent the night at anyone else's house.

Middle school was rough because everyone was trying to fit into newly formed friend groups. Most kids held pretty tight to their secrets, worried that the littlest revealed detail might reclassify them into an undesired group. I stood as an outsider to all these groups, watching the intermingling of people as they tried out each clique and eventually settled for wherever they felt the most comfortable. My understanding of nonverbal cues was learned largely from being an observer rather than a participant. Even when the typical bullying behavior crept in, I was excluded from those antics, largely unseen as a potential target. I desperately wanted to be included, even if it meant being the brunt of the abuse.

Once high school started, gossip became a big thing. I lived vicariously through the stories I heard day in and day out, wishing for the chance to be one of the normal girls just for one day and be the subject of the story rather than just an observer. Over time, the stories became juicer, and I became obsessed with learning every new detail. School was like a daily soap opera, and I needed my fix. Each new piece brought more intrigue to the plot, and it became an obsession to get the newest tidbits before anyone else. I made excuses to go to the bathroom multiple times throughout the day, just so I could stand on the toilet in the hopes of hearing a bit of gossip from the girls who came in. Once, I even snuck into the boy's locker room and hid in an empty locker to try and get dirt from their perspective. As I iced the aches and pains I acquired sitting in a squished locker for six hours, I thought enough was enough. Really, what was so interesting about everyone else anyway?

But I couldn't stop. I was addicted. I skipped class more and more to get the latest news by whatever means possible, sometimes just sitting in a random corner to scroll through social media posts and commit them to memory. My grades slipped, and I was called to the office by the assistant principal. I was required to take a study hall to complete my homework and try to improve my grades. Hah, if they only knew. Study hall was the prime spot for my obsession. They were doing me a favor. Hardly anyone did homework in study hall. It was just an excuse for gossiping, playing on your phone, and hanging out. I could leisurely lounge at my table like a cat curled up in a window seat on a bright, sunny day and listen in on several conversations at once, filling in the missing details of the various pieces of gossip I had already heard that week. How magnificent.

IRRITATION

"Why is your door locked? Come and open it at once."

I was able to crawl out from the grips of my mind's cocoon well enough to stand up and open my bedroom door.

"The principal called me at work today. Said something about bad grades and a mandatory study hall. I expect more from you." Blah blah blah blah.

I turned my back to my mom and settled back on my bed for her lecture. At least I was getting some attention. Without a call to work, she never would have noticed my grades at all, no matter how many messages appeared on her voicemail or in her emails. At work, she was forced to take the call. Otherwise, how would it look to her co-workers if she didn't show concern over her daughter? She wouldn't dare do something to indicate she was a bad mother, or even a preoccupied mother, because that would reflect badly on her. That, at its heart, was the kicker. She was all about appearances, but she didn't even see me.

"Did you hear me? Did you? And what did you do to your hair?"

Pop the champagne. Blow the whistles. Mark it on the calendar. It took my mother thirteen whole days to notice I had cut my hair short and dyed it blonde. It must have been a record of some sort, making it the shortest time it took her to notice something new about me. The previous record was the stint I spent in the attic when I was in middle school. It took her nineteen days to realize I had moved most of my everyday belongings into the attic, except for my bed and dresser, and I had been spending all my evenings after school in the corner cave I made for myself. It was my version of a treehouse that I had heard my classmates talking about, and I soon realized the allure. Mom went ballistic the day she found out. She even took the next morning off work so that she could personally move all my stuff back into my bedroom and then place the attic under lock and key. Her move bewildered me at the time, making me suspect that there was something important up there. I never came across anything that seemed to warrant her concerns, but I had never explored beyond the corner I set up. I had always wanted to figure out a way to go back up in the attic to see what Mom was hiding, and as she complained to me about my blonde hair, I reminded myself that I had yet to reopen that door.

You may be wondering: How did a mother not realize where her daughter was sleeping for nineteen days in a row—or for that matter whether I was even at home for those nineteen days? Behold the essence of my mother. She was very self-absorbed and only took notice of me when she wanted me to do something for her. The night she found out I was in the attic, she had been in search of me to brush out her hair because her shoulder was getting too tired. That night, I realized just how self-centered she truly was and that I was nothing more than a convenient attendant for her needs. With that disheartening realization, I felt myself turning inward more than ever, which only deepened my depression and isolation.

I blinked my eyes, coming back to the present moment while Mom babbled on for about five straight minutes about how important it was for her to maintain a professional appearance when she was at work, and that having the assistant principal call her was unacceptable and gave a bad impression. I tuned her out again. I had heard versions of this speech before and had no interest in hearing yet another diatribe about how I should not be interfering in her life.

In her life! Last time I checked, she was the one who gave birth to me and brought me into her life in the first place. The irony was not lost on me, but she had never been one to express an understanding of irony or tragic comedy. I caught her last few sentences, including the threat that "You better not let this happen again, or there will be vast consequences." I bit the inside of my cheek to prevent myself from laughing out loud at this empty threat. Mom had never carried out any of her threatened punishments because it would have required more interaction with me and distracted her from her own life. If she would have ever carried through, I would have misbehaved intentionally just to get the negative attention.

As she walked out of my bedroom, she left me with, "I expect this study hall will pay off and you can bring those grades up because I do not want to ever be interrupted again at work by a phone call from school for any reason."

I wondered how many of her co-workers even knew I existed before today's phone call. I highly doubted there were any pictures on her desk or mementos to suggest she had a daughter. Her social calendar certainly didn't include me, and I'm sure the conservations she had with her co-workers centered around what new restaurants they had tried, what bars made the best drinks, or what travel destinations they would like to visit. In confirmation of this, I heard the sound of the door slamming behind her as she left to go out to the new martini bar in town. I could only imagine her thoughts as she left the house. "Good. That's handled. Now I can get back to my evening." What I desperately was hoping she was thinking was, "What is going on with her lately? I'm worried about her." Yet, I knew Mom was much too preoccupied with her own life to pay any attention to my struggles.

ENVIOUS

I loved study hall. I wanted desperately to make it part of my daily schedule, but how could I accomplish that? Was it as easy as talking with the guidance counselor and asking for it, or did I need to be failing a class? I didn't want to intentionally do poorly in school, but maybe simply asking to drop an elective and adding the study hall would work. I stopped by the counselors' office, but no one was there. I went to the school office, and after showing my school ID for the thousandth time, the secretary filled out the request for me and told me I would be notified soon of what the next steps would be. I got an email by the end of the day informing me that the switch had been made.

Really? That was it? They didn't want a face-to-face meeting to make sure I was okay? I guess not. It was just hit the stamp of approval and move onto the next request. No wonder I felt like no one saw me. I was simply a piece of paperwork in a large stack of busy work. I didn't linger on this for too long, though, because the school dance was in five weeks and the hallways (really the entire school and every class) were completely engrossed in all the details that surround a dance. For something like that, study hall was the best place to be.

"Is it going to be themed?"

"Should we even bother with a theme? They're usually lame anyways."

"If it is done right, a theme could be fun."

"What kind of dress should we get? Long or short?"

"It depends on what Annika is wearing. She'll set the tone for the night."

"Where do you think she'll get it from?"

"Probably that boutique in downtown Charleston that she always goes to. I think she is going this weekend actually."

"Did Annika and Kyle make up? Are they going together?"

"I haven't heard. She seems to be keeping it a secret, but honestly I don't think they ever actually broke up, and it was just a fight."

"Who is hosting the after-party?"

"Are Collin's parents going to be gone that weekend? His house is the perfect party house."

"I'll ask him in our next class. I'm sure that he's up for it."

"I'm sneaking a flask into the dance. Do you want me to get you one?"

"Yes, I definitely want one. Will you fill it for me too?"

The days and weeks ticked by, and surprise, surprise, no one had asked me to the dance. One day, I foolishly thought Tyler was going to ask. I was sitting in my new study hall class, casually pretending to read a book so I could get caught up on the latest gossip, and he came and sat down in the chair next to me. I was startled because no one ever sat next to me. I started sweating and had a thousand thoughts all at once, but all I could do was stare at him. I couldn't bring myself to speak. He glanced over and flashed his grin, his smile reaching all the way to his gorgeous, sky-blue eyes. This was it, I thought. He's going to compliment my new hair style and ask if I would go to the dance with him. But he looked past me and waved. There was Jordan, walking up behind me, and he was trying to get his attention.

How stupid could I be? He never was going to ask me. He probably never even saw me. How could I let myself think that? This was Tyler, varsity football player and good-looking charmer; of course he already had a date to the dance. And then I remembered something I had overheard from my perch on the toilet in the girls' bathroom—he was going with Samantha. How could I have forgotten such a thing? I guess I wanted a date even more than I had realized. I excused myself from the table, and he didn't even notice I had left.

I was lost in my thoughts as I entered the hallway. How could I let myself get so flustered by the thought of a date? I always thought I was above such things and was more concerned about the more meaningful aspects to life, but in a second, all those delusions had vanished. How disappointing. Maybe I had tried to trivialize the social aspects of school to avoid the painful realization of what I was missing. Maybe I was wrong about it being so shallow. Maybe it was worth more of an effort, even though all my attempts of inclusion had been thwarted in the past. How could I make it change?

And then someone opened a classroom door right into me, and I ran face-first into it, knocking me back to the reality of the moment. The student proceeded on his way, not even acknowledging he had hit me, further proving I was invisible to everyone and deepening the hurt from a moment ago at the table. But then I heard, "I saw Annika and Kyle talking right before their last class, and they seemed pretty cozy with each other," and I was hooked yet again by the allure of knowing the latest gossip.

The rumbles in the hall about Kyle and Annika ramped up in intensity. No one seemed to be able to figure out if they were together or not. Kyle was supposedly going with Hanna, leaving Annika dateless and confirming they had split, but that seemed to be a stretch. There was no conceivable way Annika would be dateless to the biggest event of the year. I overheard Madison telling a group of attentive girls that Hanna was just a ploy to make Annika jealous and Kyle wanted her back. Which, again, would mean they had split up and he was trying to make amends. Or was that just Annika's hope and Madison's fear? Madison had not been shy about sharing her desires to be Kyle's girlfriend to anyone who would listen. How could I get to the bottom of it? What connections about Hanna did I already know, and how could I ascertain if she was Kyle's date or being used as a pawn?

Even the teachers gave up trying to complete any lesson plans in the final week before the dance. The girls practiced different hair styles in class and compared dresses to make sure no one would have a duplicate. The boys compared who they were going with and how far they would get at the after-party. I coveted each new piece of information, happy that I was in study hall where most of the news worth knowing was revealed right in front of me. I was in my glory, with each little revelation almost as gratifying as the ping of a notification on my phone.

INADEQUATE

Was I going to go to the dance? Of course! There was no way I was getting behind on all of my people. If I didn't go, I would be lost on Monday. Everything would happen at the dance, and everything I spent weeks trying to piece together should all come to fruition in front of my eyes. I had to go; there simply was not a choice, despite my utter disdain for the charade of it all. Yet, I couldn't help but feel the sting of being left on the fringes yet again.

It was late Saturday afternoon, and I needed to leave soon for the dance. My mom walked by my room and noticed me putting on my shoes. She lingered at the door and asked where I was going. This was shocking as she normally didn't even notice if I was home or not. I opened my mouth before I could think and told her I was leaving for the dance in a few minutes. I instantly regretted my casual admission. The gates of motherhood opened, and she threw herself into the room, lunging for the closet and insisting I try on something "more appropriate for a dance." This was to no avail, as there was nothing in my closet that was dance attire. She stood glaring at the closet, willing for something to appear. I tried to shoo her away, but before I could escape the house, she excitedly returned from her room with a floor-length dress of black silk with a plunging V-neck.

I know my mom was all about appearances, but my first reaction was "there is no way I am wearing that dress." I much preferred the simple, navy, long-sleeve, cotton dress I was already wearing. I didn't even want to wear a dress at all, but I thought I might stand out too much if I was wearing jeans, and I figured that if was going to get the best gossip on the dance floor or in the girls' bathroom, it was important for me to blend in. I'm not sure why I worried about it; they never saw me in the past, and the dance would likely be no different, but I couldn't take that big of a chance. I relented to Mom's pleas of wearing the black dress, mainly so I could get out of the house and get to the dance on time. Once I had it on, I looked in the mirror and felt like an imposter in my own skin, but maybe it would make me feel like I was one of the normal girls once I got to the dance.

Mom started fussing over my hair, my makeup, my nails. She obviously was trying to get her daughter to arrive at the dance as a reflection of herself, and honestly, as much as the very idea repulsed me, there was a part of me that was thrilled. I had sought Mom's undivided attention on many occasions without success, and I finally had her doting over me—me! I sat on the vanity stool in her room and allowed her to do her fussing. I watched her actions in the mirror, trying to get my hair to lay just right with a curl, tucking her fingers along my ear, brushing the blush across my cheeks. I started to feel a sense of warmth and love in my heart. I felt a smile starting to emerge on my face, but in an instant, it evaporated into thin air.

"There," she said. "I think I've succeeded in making you look sort of pretty. Much better than the way you normally look." If that was the first time I had heard one of her cutting remarks, I would have dissolved in a puddle of tears and run from the room, but I had grown up with her off-the-cuff insults and disapproval. I gritted my teeth and nodded, fighting back the moisture threatening to spill from the corner of my eye. My steel resolve returned, and her remarks slid off me like a fish off a hook, though I still felt the sharp prongs. I half-smiled at Mom in the mirror, ducked my head, and told her I needed to leave or I would be late.

I grabbed my shoes and clutch from my bed and headed out the door, pausing for the slightest moment on the doormat of the porch. Did I actually want to go through with this? I felt so uncomfortable and self-conscious as I looked at my reflection in the door window. Who was this? I didn't recognize her in the least. Maybe, just maybe, this person I didn't know was someone my peers would accept. Would I have to learn how to be this person day in and day out to accomplish my goal of inclusion? The weight of that possibility hung in the air as I took one last look in the window and left for the dance.

EUPHORIC

The dance. This was it. The social structure for the rest of the semester would hinge on the events of tonight. I stood in the corner of the gym, scoping out the scene and determining the best vantage points for overhearing gossip. My main objective was to determine if Kyle and Annika were back together or if it was a façade for the night. The whole school was talking about Kyle's last-minute drop of Hanna as a date, but she didn't seem that upset about it. Based on her casual attitude, I doubted she ever was planning on going with him. It seemed like Kyle had made it up to get Annika's attention and Hanna had been in on it the whole time. At least, that was the buzz around school for the last couple days, and I was determined to discover the truth.

As I took everything in, I heard whispering amongst some nearby students but couldn't make out what they were saying. I tried to move closer without being obvious. I was just close enough to start grabbing bits of conversation about a new girl when Annika walked in. All previous conversations were halted as everyone raved about her dress, her shoes—really, just her. She looked like the princess of the ball, and in all fairness, she was the princess of the ball—and the entire school, for that matter. She knew it and played the part well. She flashed her perfect smile to everyone as she made her way to the center of the dance floor. Unaccompanied.

First, I was astounded, then puzzled. Why wasn't her date escorting her in? His status would instantly be secured by escorting the most popular girl at school into the gym. Where was he? And where was Kyle? My eyes scanned the gym, but I couldn't find him anywhere in the crowd. This didn't add up. Maybe Annika was upset about the jealousy stunt he had attempted with Hanna. Maybe she had refused to come as his date, or maybe she really did want to be done with him. Once she hit the center of the dance floor, the crowd surrounded her. Her coming without a date was a moot point, as everyone wanted to dance with her or be near her. I slowly made my way through the crowd, trying to absorb the essence of the night. Tonight I looked like I belonged, thanks to Mom, so maybe I could fool myself into believing that I was actually one of them.

For a moment, I was blissfully happy. I couldn't recall the last time I had felt this light. I was in the middle of the dance floor and high on the feeling that I was included. I felt normal. Well, as normal as I could feel without anyone acknowledging my presence. I didn't even get bumped into, didn't get "accidentally" grabbed by the hormone-strung teenage boys, didn't get caught up in the classic party dances. I was frankly avoided as if I were a column of the gym structure rather than a person. Tonight, though, none of that mattered. I was taken up by the music, the atmosphere, and a sense that I was part of their crowd.

As I made a stealthy departure from the floor (which wasn't even necessary, since no one knew I was there), I overheard Tyler say, "Who is the girl in the black dress?" His friend, Jordan, replied, "I heard that she's from another school, but no one seems to know her name." I looked around to see if I could spot this new girl who had gained the attention of none other than Tyler, but I couldn't locate anyone in a black dress. I made three quick sweeps around the gym and didn't see anyone whom I didn't already know, so I moved on to the girls' bathroom to try and find this mystery girl. I was feeling left out, not knowing who she was, and it seemed like she was gaining more attention by the second. My anxiety was climbing that I would miss out. And of greatest importance, she had caught Tyler's eye.

I pretended to fix my lipstick in the mirror as Madison was talking about how she planned to steal Kyle away from Annika at the after-party and declare him as hers. YES!!! The juiciest piece of gossip yet, and I heard it just in time. But what if they wouldn't let me into the party to see what was happening? I started to orchestrate a plan because I HAD to be at that party. Even though none of the kids from school had ever invited me to their house before, I was determined to go. I figured that since no one had noticed me all night, I could just slip in with the crowd as they went into the house. That would be Option A. If that failed, I would figure out an Option B.

I went back to the gym to bask in one last ray of happiness from the dance floor. I knew that meant I was risking arriving late to the after-party, but I couldn't pass this up. Who knew when I would ever feel like this again? As the last song finished that I dare partake in, I heard Tyler again asking about the girl in the black dress. I only saw one girl in a black dress besides me, but she was making out with her date from another school in the corner of the gym. I couldn't imagine he meant her. Then it occurred to me. Could he actually be curious about me? Maybe Mom's efforts had paid off, as much as it repulsed me that I had to pretend to be someone I was not to get his attention, but it worked. If this version of me held Tyler's interest, it might be worth maintaining the charade as a long-term strategy.

I started to flaunt the dance moves that I had learned from TikTok and YouTube and tried to make eye contact with him. I felt a thrill as he returned my gaze, but then Jordan rushed up to him and said they had to catch their ride for the after-party. The after-party! I was so absorbed with my flirtation with Tyler that I almost forgot about the need to arrive at the right moment to blend in with the crowd. I took one more glance into his fabulous eyes and disappeared from the gym. Even he would not distract me from the task at hand.

REELING

I hastily changed into jeans and a baggy long sleeve T-shirt before leaving the school. I felt like myself again and could proceed to the next phase of the evening without the possibility, as had just occurred on the dance floor, of being distracted from my mission. Option A for getting into the after-party was way easier than I thought it would be. I just followed a group of people through the door. I strategically placed myself in the upstairs closet next to the bathroom, which I figured would be the best place to eavesdrop and hear the best gossip from practically everyone at the party.

The first contestant entered the bathroom.

"I have to get out of this dress. I starved myself for three days to zip into it. It was worth it, but it has to go. Do you have a joint?"

"No, but I have this instead."

"What is it?"

"Cocaine. Way better than a joint. It will give you the best night of your life."

I never really considered drugs, even though they were prevalent around me. I saw drug deals in the hallways every day, but the teachers turned a blind eye. Weed, cocaine, even heroin seemed so common that the novelty had quickly worn off. I tried weed a few times because the concept sounded appealing and I was hoping it would ease my depression, mellow me out, and allow me to go through the day adrift, but I quickly realized that I did not like its effect. It made me anxious, paranoid, and unable to focus. With something as "mild" as weed having such a dramatic effect, I was scared off from trying any other drugs.

Tangent aside, I could not quite make out who was in the bathroom, and I desperately wanted to know. One of the girls sounded like Annika, but there was no way it was her. Why would she need cocaine to have a good night? I didn't have the chance to find out. They had already left. I chastised myself for getting caught up in my own thoughts and possibly missing the key detail to the puzzle.

Second contestant: "Quick, before anyone realizes you left. Help me with my zipper."

"No one knows we're gone, and even if they do, who cares?"

"Kyle will care. He can't know I'm with you. It will completely ruin everything."

"Kyle? What the hell? I thought you were going to have sex with me?"

"I am going to have sex with you, you idiot, but I don't want to be with you."

I was flipping out in my mind but suppressed myself from jumping up and down. That must be Annika, but who was the guy? I leaned forward to hear their voices more distinctly but stupidly slipped and got tangled in the vacuum hose, knocking my body against the wall. The thumping startled them.

"What was that? Forget it. I'm out of here."

I heard the boy start to leave and thought that I would cleverly crack the door and sneak a peek in the hallway to see who it was, but I hesitated just in time to hear, "Madison, can I interest you in a drink?"

"Umm, sure, I guess," she responded.

Finally, I was getting some names and could start to fill in some of the details of the last few encounters.

"What are you doing up here anyways, Collin?"

"Um, well, I just was helping Annika with a stuck zipper on her special party dress as she called it. She said that it's too big of a night to only have one dress."

THANK YOU!! THANK YOU, COLLIN!! He had just provided all the clues I needed to figure out that it was indeed Annika who had starved herself to get into the dress. She wanted the joint and maybe was doing cocaine tonight. And the biggest secret of all, he was just in the bathroom with Annika about to have sex with her while she was trying to still get back with Kyle. But if she was willing to be with Collin, did she even like Kyle or was that just for appearances' sake? This was turning into quite the little love triangle, but who was playing who? My mind started spinning with the possibilities. I was satisfied with accomplishing my mission for the night and could happily go home if I could just get the opportunity to get out of the closet unnoticed.

I had to wait a few minutes, but finally there seemed to be a clearance in the hallway. I emerged from the closet and was closing the door when I saw Tyler coming up the steps. I wanted him to recognize me as myself, now that I was out of the black dress and wasn't trying to put on any charade, but he walked straight past without a second glance or recognition of the connection we had shared just hours earlier. Even his dismissiveness wasn't enough to ruin my mood, though. I rushed home to take notes on everything I had learned tonight. I went to my room, basking in a glorious feeling of success and too excited to sleep.

If only I had someone I could share all of this with and help me weave all the plot lines together. I wanted a friend to challenge my thinking and help me develop a more complex web of possibilities. The realization of my loneliness was like a slap across my cheek. My high started to wear off, just like any high does, and familiar feelings of isolation and despair returned. How quickly my pleasure and success turned to utter failure. I stripped my face of the last remnants of Mom's makeup, put away her dress, wrapped myself in a blanket, and embraced the darkness with the image of Tyler walking past me playing on repeat. His rejection of me just being myself seared into my heart and could not be undone.

DISBELIEF

Why was I going to such great strides to blend in with crowd? My experience at the dance proved that no one knew who I was as my true self or would bother to give me a second glance anyway. It wouldn't matter if I ran down the hallway naked; they still would not notice. My new plan be the most obnoxious person I could, which would force people to take notice.

On Thursday, I decided to head to school with new attire. I left my leggings and oversized long sleeve t-shirt behind and instead donned a skirt with fishnet stockings and heels. For balance, I had on a button-down shirt with the top two buttons undone. I didn't even recognize the girl staring back at me in the mirror. All courtesy of my mom's closet—not to imply that she dresses like this; she doesn't. I just created a look using some of her things, trying to mimic what I have seen in the hallways and movies. I actually put makeup on, using what I learned from YouTube tutorials. I think it was at least passable and not too clownish. I felt awkward and uncomfortable in my own skin but told myself it would be worth it. I would be allowed into their club as a normal high school teenager. I left home without Mom even noticing the drastic change in my wardrobe selection. I hesitated only slightly. If Mom didn't notice, would anyone else? I shrugged it off and headed to school, convincing myself that I could do it. This bold move would pay off. It worked at the dance for a brief moment, it would work again.

No one turned their head to look while I strutted, or at least didn't fall, down the hall to my locker. In my head, I was trying to emulate everything I observed everyone else doing. I leisurely opened my locker, leaned against the edge, and took my time getting ready for the first bell. Could you believe it? Not one person noticed the new me. Even the two kids with the lockers on either side of me grabbed their books without a second glance. Are you freaking kidding me?!!?!? Why did I go through any of these painstaking preparations and make myself into a person I didn't even recognize? They were just in a hurry, I told myself and deliberately took my time walking to class, trying to make eye contact with everyone on my route. A few students held my gaze for a brief second, but just as quickly moved past me. Not one person pointed and whispered, nodded their head, whistled, or gave any indication that they noticed anything different about me.

I went to my first class and purposely tripped through the door to draw attention to my entrance. No one glanced up or even seemed to hear the commotion. I sulkily took my usual seat, and the teacher started class. I yearned to hear my peers' mumblings of appreciation, curiosity, astonishment, or at the very least disgust and disbelief. Nothing. The teacher didn't even give me the decency of raising her eyebrow at my new wardrobe. I was in sheer shock, sitting in my chair in a daze without hearing a word the teacher said and only being startled by the bell. Even then, I was frozen in my seat, unwilling to move, unwilling to accept that all the morning's efforts had been in vain.

The second class and third class were identical to the first, without a single acknowledgement of the different attire or makeup. Had the extreme wardrobes over the years dulled the teachers' reactions to such antics? By lunch, I deemed my efforts a failure. I grabbed a sweatshirt from my locker to cover my button-down shirt and ditched the fishnet stockings for the remainder of my classes. Besides the heels, I almost felt back to myself again.

DEVIOUS

Provocative dress did nothing to catch anyone's attention, even though I kept up the efforts for an entire week, changing it up and upping the ante with each passing day. The only thing I accomplished was making myself sit uncomfortably through five long days and develop blisters from all the different footwear.

I needed to try a new strategy. What should the next thing be that might possibly catch someone's attention and help me feel a sense of belonging in their club? Why did I so desperately want to be noticed and included in this circle? I couldn't seem to find the answer but continued striving for this goal. I guess it had something to do with how light I felt while I was in the middle of the dance floor a few weeks ago and how desperately I wanted to feel like that again. It seemed shallow, but I didn't care. I played the dance floor sequence in my mind time and time again, feeling the joy in my chest keep me afloat during the last few days. That in and of itself was the answer—the precise reason why I wanted to be in their inner circle. I wanted the opportunity to have a source of happiness every single day. It would be worth the sacrifice of my own self-identity. I wanted to be seen, I wanted to be included, and I wanted to matter.

I started concocting my next plan. I was always an average student, staying in the middle of the pack for grades, mainly because I was too preoccupied with my gossip addiction to do well. These average students coasted without much attention from the teachers because the were doing just fine. But maybe I could become the belligerent student, the one who all the teachers hated and often rallied other students to take part in their antics. This could be my next move, but would it draw the attention of my peers or just the teachers? Would I even be able to get the other kids to participate? They had yet to see me. I didn't really have interest in causing unrest for the teachers if it wouldn't bring me closer to my goal. I actually enjoy learning, but somehow this had not been enough to survive my high school career. I saw a few other students get engrossed in their studies, taking advanced classes, being in math club, debate, school newspaper, and so forth. I'm not sure what kept me from trying that pathway. Probably a fear I wasn't smart enough to pull it off—or worse, even those groups would reject me, and I would fail yet again. The fear of rejection likely kept me from the very inclusion I sought.

Instead, I wondered, could I make the students hate me? Attention was attention, right? I've learned that over and over and over with my mom and peers alike. But how could I incite hate among those who didn't even know me?

Pulling pranks? I was never very good at that sort of thing, but I could probably get better by watching videos on YouTube. From what I could see, though, the victims of the pranks got over them pretty quickly and spectators didn't find them funny for more than a few seconds. It didn't seem worth it to go through so much trouble for something that would only temporarily annoy people and would probably not have a long-term impact. I needed something more sustainable to create a new identity. Purposefully being mean? That would be quite out of character for me, but I had tried other personas to meet my agenda in the past. I could do it again. I started brainstorming ideas that might generate enough impact to cause everyone in the school to care.

Then it hit me. I already knew all their inner secrets. It was time for me to put that information to use for my own benefit. I was going to air everyone's secrets that I'd kept hidden in the labyrinth of my brain.

Yes, yes this could work! It would definitely draw attention as everyone tried to figure out the truth behind each secret. I would be either the pariah for broadcasting gossip all over the school or the heroine for bringing down Annika. I recently realized through my overhead conversations that a few "close friends" were secretly quite jealous of her, spreading rumors behind her back, and they might enjoy seeing her knocked down a peg or two. I would take the weekend to map out who was in each of my classes and create a masterful plan by revealing little tidbits strategically throughout the day to get everyone bent out of shape. This would force them to take notice of who was bringing all the whispered rumors out into the open and would make them finally see me. Of everything, this was the route most plausible to be a success. As I thought about my plan coming to fruition, I couldn't help but smile like the cat who had just caught the mouse.

SATISFIED

Monday morning arrived. It was going to be epic. I woke up early and got ready for school, running through my plan in my head. Mom stopped by my room. What?!? I usually was eager for her attention, but today of all days! *Ugh ... not now, Mom. You are definitely going to hamper my good mood.*

She paused at the doorway, and I side-glanced at her, not even turning my body. She opened her mouth to say something but held back. She shook her head a little and continued down the hallway. What was that? I chalked it up to just another day of her ignoring me and continuing her passiveness towards me.

Today was the end of being left in the shadows. I would no longer be ignored by my peers.

I stopped by my locker quickly, eager to get to my first class. I took my seat and leaned over to Kyle, who was sitting next to me, not even caring that he had never given me the time of day. "Hey, Kyle. I heard Collin tried to hook up with Annika at the party a few weeks ago."

He looked up astonished, slightly pale. "Where did you hear that?"

I slyly looked at him. "I have my sources. Sounds like it got a little heated when he helped her with the zipper on her dress."

I saw the paleness in his face turn abruptly to anger as the possibilities ran through his brain. Yes! Success! The seed was planted, and bonus—he looked at me and even acknowledged me.

The bell rang, and Kyle bolted from the classroom door. I smiled to myself. This might be even better than collecting the gossip just for myself. I started to imagine the disarray about to ensue throughout the day merely by sharing truths with strategic people.

Second period. Kyle was in this class too, and I saw him whispering to multiple people. He appeared nervous. Part of me felt a pang of regret, but then he made eye contact with me, and I forgot about that and started to melt. He saw me. I was starting to be seen for the first time during high school, and it was intoxicating. He was talking to Tyler, the football stud I had a crush on. Kyle gave a little head nod toward me, and Tyler turned to look. Oh, man. This was great. I tried to play it cool, like I hadn't just given Kyle the worst news of the year. Tyler began to get up from his chair, but the teacher started class. He hesitated and then sat down again.

When the bell rang at the end of class, I quickly headed out the door. I needed to hurry to the other end of the building to give myself enough time to unleash my next truth. I rushed past people and heard someone shouting behind me, "Hey, you, in the navy shirt." They couldn't be talking to me, could they? I looked back and caught a glimpse of Tyler. He seemed to be trying to wave me down. I paused briefly, wanting nothing more than to rush back toward him, but the next phase of my plan had to be set in motion before it was too late. How embarrassing and disappointing that as much as I condemned the superficial desires and antics of my peers, I was not above them. I nearly responded just as eagerly and predicably without pause to Tyler's beckoning.

In my next class, I slid into my chair abruptly and startled Madison. I blurted out, "Hey, Madison, Annika tried to hook up with Collin at the party, and Kyle is pissed. Now is your chance to get Kyle if you want him." At first, she didn't even seem to hear me, and then the realization of what I said seemed to sink in. I saw her mind start to spin, and she looked at me, gripping my forearm. "Are you sure?" Hearing the hope in her voice. I simply nodded and turned around. All through class, Madison kept trying to glean more details from me, whispering over my shoulder. This was heaven. I was the one with the information that everyone wanted to know. My voice mattered. I fed Madison just enough information to keep her curious and left an opening for more follow-up questions. By the end of class, she was eating out of the palm of my hand, just like pigeons pecking at the morsels thrown on a sidewalk. This was better than I hoped for.

BITTER

The hallways were buzzing.

"Did you hear?"

"Kyle is mad and looking for Collin."

"I heard Annika and Collin talking in the back hallway."

"Madison was chatting Kyle up at lunch, heavy."

I stood at my locker and absorbed this feeling. I had caused this buzz. I was finally going to be recognized as the one who knew the inside scoop and would be sought after for gossip by everyone. I smiled and relaxed. I had finally, *finally* found my niche and decided I would strive even harder to be up to date with everyone's secrets so I would always be the go-to source. I seemed to have Madison, Kyle, and maybe even Tyler giving credence to my information. The high that I had been searching for had finally arrived. This was better than the dance. This was everything I had hoped for and more. I didn't even know it could feel this good, this normal. I was swept up in the theatrics of high school life, like everyone else, and for the first time, I even felt included in their club.

I was in the middle of basking in my glory when my bubble burst into pieces. I saw Tyler walking down the hallway, certain he was coming to me to get the "true story" I had leaked to Kyle this morning, but he stopped about six feet away from my locker. I overheard him talking and absolutely could not believe my ears. He was telling someone that Kyle heard from Madison that Annika was hooking up with Collin. The audacity. What in the actual hell? He was ruining my plan, my carefully orchestrated plan to put myself on the map and establish my place in this crazy high school world. I slammed my locker and barged my way through a few people because I was not about to let someone else get credit for all of this beautiful chaos. I needed this to work. It had to work because I had no other moves.

Out of sheer exasperation and anger, I approached Tyler and boldly tapped him on the shoulder. "You know I'm the one who told Kyle about Annika and Collin. You saw me."

He scarcely glanced down at me and retorted, "Yeah, but I don't know you who are. No one knows you. It's better to say that Madison started the rumor because then people are going to believe it." He sauntered away with a sneer on his face.

Dejected. Worse than dejected. He saw me for a brief moment and, just as swiftly, disregarded me as a person.

RESENTMENT

I went home and collapsed on my bed. I could not move. I could not even think. I laid there as if in an utter abyss, staring at my ceiling. How could I be so delusional to think I would suddenly become the most trusted gossip source at the school and gain instant street cred? Maybe I had implemented my plan too abruptly. Maybe I should have waited. What would be the point anyway? I had been trying to get noticed in school for the last two-and-a-half years. Waiting would not have done any good. I would never be known no matter what I did. Maybe that was it. Maybe I needed to do something truly shocking to make my mark. That's when it occurred to me that my absence might be the best way to confirm my existence.

I started to consider the option. What was the point of my life anyway? No one at school saw me, or even if they did see me, they decided I didn't matter. My own mother didn't see me. Did I even see myself?

Maybe the world would be better without me?

I had not really contemplated suicide before, but lying on my bed, I thought it seemed like an excellent option. Of course I had heard of people doing it and saw it in the news headlines, but it was never in the forefront of my mind. I had never personally been affected by someone who had completed the act. But why shouldn't I do it? No one would even care, and ironically, I would make myself better known in the process. The news of my demise would ensure that everyone at school would know who I was.

I went back to school a few days later, having managed to get myself out of bed and changed into clean clothes. I had skipped a few days to recover from the complete failure of my gossip unleashing plan. If I was lucky, maybe I had become the laughingstock of the school. Some kids might be talking about what a failure I was, which at least would mean I was noticed, even though it was in a backwards way from what I had intended. I returned, though, to no change. Literally no change at all. They still didn't know who I was. Even Tyler, who spoke to me after the gossip bomb I detonated at the start of the week, didn't give me any sideways glances during our classes together—not a hint of acknowledgement that I even existed. My elaborate plans were such a waste. I had accomplished nothing.

There was still plenty of buzz about the big reveal at the beginning of the week, and everyone was scrambling to figure out the nuances of the intertwined relationships. I heard whispers and many half-truths being spread around. No one had put all of it together yet. I intentionally had left them hanging that day, so I could be the one to earn the accolades for setting it all straight. But I found myself not caring anymore. Even when I was in the middle of the action, Tyler proved I would never secure a place in reputable gossip circles, despite all of my efforts. I'll admit that seeing them scurry around trying to fit all the pieces together was a bit satisfying. It served them right. Maybe it would help them understand what it felt like to be left out of something, like I had felt countless times over the years. Maybe it would even make them question their status at school. That's something I never had to do. I had no status—never had and never would.

In the bathroom, I overheard murmurings that Annika might not be going to college in the fall; the rumor was she might be pregnant. Typically, this delicious detail would have thrown me into a delightful frenzy. My mind would have been working overtime to figure out how this new information fit into the events from the dance. I would have created plot lines in my head and enacted plans to get all the pieces of the story together so I could determine who the father might be, or whether she would even have the baby. Today, I barely even glanced over to see who was talking. I was apathetic to one of the biggest scandals of the year. What was wrong with me? With gossip no longer able to sustain my days, what would I do now? I needed something else to make my days matter, but what? How could I find something that aligned with my higher aspirations? Did I even have any goals? When was the last time I hoped for anything other than being included into the school's inner circle?

The more I observed, the more I realized how superficial my peers' life view was and how they no longer interested me. Everything I had strived to become a part of was such a waste of a life and a complete lie. I wanted more. I despised my mom for years because of her superficial take on life and her deliberate avoidance of anything that mattered, namely me. I yearned for a sense of belonging, a sense of inclusion, and a sense that I mattered to someone. I felt like I was searching and searching for something that would always elude me. I retreated within myself even more, and the gossip surrounding me served as a reminder of everything I was trying to escape and truthfully starting to disdain. I couldn't seem to find my way.

I was lost without any foothold to anchor me.

DESOLATION

The days and weeks blended together. Nearly two months drifted by, and I was still incredibly lost. Indescribably, utterly, staring-into-the-abyss lost. I spent many days in bed, unable to move. I didn't get up to eat, drink, or barely even use the bathroom. I couldn't tell you the last time I showered. Did I even eat yesterday? If my mom stopped in my room, I didn't notice. There weren't even messages from the school wondering where I had been; they didn't miss me. I was nothing to them—to anyone.

I gazed up at the ceiling for hours, counting how many times the fan blades went around or watching a fly crawl from one end of the wall to the other. TV and music used to serve as a comfort during my mood swings, but now they had a new purpose of drowning out the self-deprecating voices in my head.

Nothing motivated me, nothing interested me, and nothing made me want to move from my lair. My room took on a distinct odor of stale sweat, dust, and remnants of untouched food, but I didn't care. Hell, I hardly even noticed it. It just became a new layer of my being.

There was no point to my days. Each one drifted into the next without me even being aware of the time passing.

I might as well have been dead. Yet I had no desire or ambition to act on this notion either. It would take too much effort to devise a plan to end it and way too much effort to have the motivation to act on a plan. What a waste of a person, a life. I was stuck.

RELIEF

I started drinking by accident really. Using alcohol was something I always felt to be pointless, but all my days seemed pointless now, so what did it matter? It started on a whim, when I journeyed out of my room for some crackers and found a plate of my mom's leftovers from the previous night next to her glass of wine. That first glass helped make my day a little bit easier. I even decided to shower. The next morning, I went downstairs to see if she had left another one on the counter from the night before. I finished her glass and then polished off the half bottle next to the sink. It made me feel a floating dissociation from my surroundings, allowing me to get through the day in my own little world and yet still be functional. This could work. I could get by like this. The faintest glimmer of a step forward.

Within a few days, I felt like I could return to school. I went back and confirmed that I was never missed. Teachers didn't reach out in concern about where I had been or talk to me about make-up work or suggest a visit with the guidance counselor. My peers continued to ignore me, but at least I was out of bed and into my normal schedule again. I was existing, but just barely. I would fly under the radar until I finished high school. But then what? I had no idea what I wanted to do after high school, and nothing seemed to be pushing me closer to finding an answer. I just knew that finishing high school was of paramount importance and life would magically get better once that piece was complete. Or at least I yearned for it to be true.

Soon the wine in the morning wasn't enough to get me through the entire school day, so I started taking vodka along to school in a water bottle. Teachers and the other students had no clue; it was hidden in plain sight. I even took flavored vodka and was ready to pass it off as Crystal Light or an energy drink, but no one even asked what I was drinking. They didn't give a shit—story of my life. The days flew by now, and I even found humor in my classes. I found myself laughing out loud at the teachers' lame attempts of dry humor. In chemistry, I found myself in a fit of giggles and thought I might pee my pants when Annika got called out by the teacher for a disruptive conversation with Madison. No wonder people drank alcohol so commonly; it made life so much easier and funnier. I was enjoying school a little bit, or at least not detesting it like before. I should have tried this ages ago.

I found a whole other set of kids at school I had previously been oblivious to. The drinkers. Once you were a drinker, you could easily spot another one despite how covert they thought they were being. I wondered if this could be my new niche, my group, somewhere I might belong unexpectedly, but a group nonetheless. At lunch one day, I sat down next to a fellow student, Dawn, who I presumed was having a liquid lunch like myself. As I had not attempted any similar lunch encounters in the past, I credited the alcohol for my courage. I introduced myself and attempted small talk to no avail. She cold-shouldered me hard. I mean, really hard, to the point that I finally had to leave the table. How rude, but yet another example of my being excluded. I wondered if she was struggling through high school using alcohol as a crutch too, or if that was something unique to me.

After the lunch table incident, I normally would have given up, but Dawn's behavior had piqued my curiosity. Surely, there were other students using alcohol to soothe their pain and mask their internal struggles. I just needed to find one like me, and we could be in this together. I began seeking out anyone I thought might be relying on alcohol, being on the lookout for some of my own tricks that I used to hide my drinking. I surmised correctly on several occasions, but very few of them wanted to engage in conversation. My instinct of their internal strife must be spot-on for them to deflect so much. The "popular" crowd was intent on informing everyone of their drunken adventures and fun, using it to help gain attention in the moment, so why was it so hard for kids who were using it as a crutch to form a bond with each other?

FEAR

Then it happened. A guy named Adam, whom I had tried to talk to earlier in the week, approached me. When we talked earlier, he had affirmed that he drank regularly throughout the school day, but he didn't continue the conversation with me, so I had dismissed him as an option for a cohort. But here he was. I had just closed my locker after refilling my "water bottle" from my secret stash, and he was leaning on the other side. I jumped, taken aback that someone had approached me first. He asked what I was drinking, and wanting to sound cool but sly at the same time, I simply said, "Vodka with Sprite."

He replied just as simply, "Cool. Why don't you and I skip the last class of the day?"

All I could do was stare. Had I heard correctly? He wanted to hang out with me? Seriously?

He started walking away and looked back over his shoulder, "Are you coming or what?"

I fumbled with my bag slightly as I eagerly started following him. Not one teacher tried to stop us as we went out the back doors of the school. I couldn't believe it was that easy. Why didn't I try this in the past? Affirmation that no one cares at school! But, at last, I was noticed by a peer, and a boy at that! I was going to finally make a friend and bond with a kindred spirit who also feel lost in the drama of high school. We walked across the parking lot, and he parted a fence behind the maintenance building, providing just enough space for us to sneak through. I could tell he had been here in the past; he knew exactly where to go. Once on the other side, I felt free for a brief moment before all hell broke loose and a new definition of terror unfolded.

He grabbed my arms and pinned them to either side of me, pushing me up against the fence, which was conveniently covered with greenery. I tried to laugh it off and told him to stop joking around—that I thought we were just going to get drunk and ditch class. His sickening laugh, with a sliver of mockery, made shivers go down my spine and the hair on the back of my neck rise an inch. This was bad news. How could I have been so dumb? He didn't want to be my friend; he wanted to use me for his own desires. Even further proof of how desperate I was for attention; I never saw the warning signs that were staring me in my face.

I needed to think fast to get out of this escalating situation. My eyes darted around, looking for any possible means of escape. Would I be able to outrun him if I got loose from his grip? I wasn't certain and didn't want to piss him off, possibly turning my precarious situation into something worse. What could I use for a weapon to protect myself if he became violent? I thought my best bet would be to find a way back through the fence where I might be spotted by a school maintenance worker or another student. Adam seemed to know what he was doing, though; he had definitely had other girls in this exact position before, and he wasn't wasting any time on niceties. He knew the window of opportunity was short.

"You think that I'll just let you go without some sort of return fee?"

Objectified. I wasn't a person to him. I was a measly tool to meet his ends. The alcohol started to revolt in my stomach, or maybe it was just the absolute disgust I felt for Adam and other guys like him. Then I realized that I could use this to my advantage. A plan took shape in my brain, and I felt like I might have a chance to break free before he could go any further. While I collected my thoughts, I played along, allowing him to stroke my hair behind my ear and kiss my neck. The whole time, I inched back toward the fence opening. When I was as close as I could manage, feeling the edge of the fence by the post at my fingertips and not wanting his hands on me any further second, I started to gag myself. I pushed him away and told him I was going to be sick. I joked that I must have had too much to drink today and held my stomach, starting to heave and gag.

It was working. He backed away and shouted, "Don't puke on my shoes." Just as he turned away from me to avoid the potential puke field, I bolted for the fence opening, clearing it but snagging my shirt sleeve on the edge. I felt the sleeve rip but kept running, not daring to look back. I ran faster than I had ever run before. I didn't know if I would be able to make it all the way back to the school without him catching me, so I opted for the maintenance shed instead, figuring one of the men would be inside and willing to help. Thankfully the door was open, and I was able to burst through just as Adam grabbed my arm. Fortunately, there was a worker immediately inside the door, who assessed the situation by taking one look at my terrified face and swiftly removed Adam's hands off my arm. Adam bolted. I was nothing to him. He would try again with someone else. I crumpled into the nearby chair and started vomiting for real; no need for pretense this time.

The worker backed away from me as I puked, but at least he gave me some paper toweling and escorted me back to the school. He took me directly to the nurse's office, happy to dispose of me as someone else's problem. That was perfectly fine by me. I was safe, thanks to him. He had led me to the safety I needed at that precise moment. I held his eyes for one more second before he left the doorway, trying to convey how thankful I was for his assistance. For some odd reason, I got the impression that I might not have been the first girl he had helped out of a similar situation. He had figured out what was happening in mere seconds, and that was enough to make Adam disappear as quick as the sly fox that he was.

DESPAIR

I assured the nurse I was okay, but I wanted to rest until the end of the school day. I was buying time. Not that I thought Adam would come back to the school, but just in case he was lurking somewhere in the hallways or outside waiting for me to emerge, I thought it was best not to walk around by myself. I lay down and had a snack, trying to settle my stomach as my mind raced through possible alternate endings to this afternoon's debacle. I was frustrated and furious with myself. I had been sloppy with my self-awareness and safety based on the mere suggestion of a possible friendship. I didn't even really think my alcohol use that day had been much of a factor; it was purely my own desperation for inclusion. My goal had been to get attention, but certainly not like this. I had no interest in being used for my body; it wasn't an option I wanted to use to get friends. I was so repulsed by the thought that I felt like I might vomit again. I needed to leave. I wanted the comfort of my own bedroom in order to reset. Before I could even tell the nurse I was ready to go home, the final bell of the day rang. I rushed into the hallways and out to the parking lot. I did a quick scan for Adam, didn't see him, so I ran home as fast as I could.

I dashed up the stairs, threw my backpack on my bed, kicked my shoes off, and hurried into the bathroom. Turning the shower to the hottest setting, I stood under the water and let out tears of anger, frustration, anguish, and fear. Today I let myself down. I stood under the stream until the water grew cold, and then I shut it off. I grabbed a towel, wrapped myself up, and sat on the edge of the tub, absorbing the steam until it faded from the bathroom. Today I had such a close call. I had let myself down. I felt like a failure. Exhausted, I put on my cozy pajama pants and crawled into bed, welcoming the soft sheets and thick comforter, and allowing myself to get lost in its embrace. I tried to get my mind to stop and rest for the night. Tomorrow would be another day.

I awoke the next morning and felt hollow. If I couldn't even count on myself, how could I ever connect with or count on anyone else? What was the purpose of even going on? How disappointing. I needed some solace. I heard Mom leave for work, so I went to the kitchen to make myself a drink. This was certainly much earlier in the day than I ever had started in the past, but today was unique. I needed a boost. I needed to make life easier to cope with, and alcohol had been the only thing that had helped with that so far. But there was a problem. A big frickin' problem. I opened the cabinet, and there was no restock from Mom's usual grocery store trip. The vodka was gone. Literally gone. That had always been my crutch. Now what?

I looked at the other liquor bottles, but I was clueless about how they tasted. Then I saw a bottle of Moscato and knew that was good, so I cracked it open and guzzled a quarter of the contents. My breathing slowed, and I calmed down. Okay. I could do this. I got ready for school, but I was running late and rushed out the door forgetting to take the Moscato with me. I was annoyed at Mom for not restocking the vodka. Was she catching on to my habit, or had she merely forgotten? I hoped there was enough in my locker stash to get me through the day, but I arrived to an empty water bottle. I felt my anxiety heighten.

As the day wore on, I became more irritable. I was distracted, I started to sweat, and I felt nauseated. Was I having a panic attack? One of the teachers stopped by my desk and told me to go to the school nurse. Since I had just been there the day before, I figured the nurse wouldn't ask too many questions and presume that I was still sick. I gradually made my way down the hallway, closing my eyes the whole way and grazing my hand along the cool, metal lockers to help lead the way, pausing once to rest my forehead against the wall. I collapsed onto the couch inside the nurse's office and soon was vomiting in the trash can, willing the room to stop spinning. I needed to go home. Again.

I left the office before the nurse even knew that I was there and somehow made it home without incident, but I have no recollection of how I achieved such a feat. I lay down on the cool bathroom floor, and the magnitude of my condition hit me with a disheartening realization. I was in withdrawal. My body had gotten so used to alcohol that it was craving it in its absence. I hurriedly went to the kitchen, bounced off the doorway, and stubbed my toe, but it was a dim pain compared to my headache. I reached for the nearest alcohol in the cabinet. Brandy. I took a big swig, gagging on the taste as it hit the back of my tongue. I sat on the floor, willing it to take effect, and within a short time, which seemed like eons, I started to feel better. My shakes went away, I stopped spinning, and my nausea improved. The realization weighed heavy on me as I sipped the brandy. I didn't want to be dependent upon anything. Yet the last few weeks were the most at peace I had been in a long time. Was I really ready to let that go? I couldn't fathom going back to being the lost and lonely girl I was just weeks ago; alcohol had given me an out. It was my friend when no one else would be.

I continued drinking to get through my days but kept a strict limit on how much I was allowed. I needed to keep a balance of just enough. Not only did I never want to experience withdrawal again, but I also couldn't risk Mom getting too wise and my supply completely vanishing. I had to switch it up to what was available and not cause alarm by emptying the bottles too quickly. I was being smart, or at least I thought I was, always drinking whatever Mom had drank the night before so she would always think she had more than she realized. This worked brilliantly, at least as far as I knew. And it allowed me to coast, bringing me up to just a high enough level from catatonic depression so that I could exist through the monotony of my days without ever compromising my judgment again.

POTENTIAL

The next Saturday, I was enjoying my usual morning alcohol allotment for the weekend to avoid withdrawal symptoms, when Mom uncharacteristically stopped in my room and asked if I wanted to join her for brunch. How odd. When was the last time we had brunch together? But I was hungry. She had ordered in French toast, eggs, and sausage from the local diner, and it smelled divine. I loaded my plate while she poured orange juice and added champagne. She told me it was called a mimosa and it was okay if I had some too. The first few sips were like bubbles dancing across the surface of my tongue and tasted incredibly delicious. I lost count of how many I drank and soon started to feel the familiar lightheadedness I experienced whenever I indulged in as much alcohol as I wanted.

I returned to my room in a tipsy state and curled up in the chair by the window. I was feeling a definite buzz and began running all kinds of scenarios through my mind. Maybe Tyler would like this flirty, more relaxed version of me; maybe I could befriend Madison; maybe playing jump rope with the line between a mild buzz and intoxication could be the answer. But then darkness invaded my thoughts, drawing ominous yet alluring shadows across my mind. *Why would anyone like this version of you better? You are worthless. You don't even know how to handle your alcohol. Maybe you should drink yourself into oblivion. No one cares about you. Even at brunch with Mom this morning, she didn't even try to have a conversation with you. You were merely a warm body sharing the room.*

I continued down this rabbit hole of darkness and despair, flirting with the recent idea of taking my own life. If I attempted suicide, it needed to be clean-cut and exact. Nothing could be left to chance. As my final act in this life, the only way suicide would mean anything was if it could be completed exactly to my plan.

Drugs were the obvious answer, as they were so prevalent around me and would be easy to come by. A drug overdose seemed like a great way to go in theory—experiencing a final high in life before slipping into slumber—but there were too many variables, and it seemed too haphazard. Killing myself would be my last chance to declare victory over the world, and I was not going to let a fumbled plan rob me of that achievement. Being altered by any substance would be unacceptable, as I wanted to be in control of my mind in my last moments on this earth. Plus, it would be way too common. "Oh, just another overdose." It would hardly even make the headlines. Not nearly shocking enough to gain attention.

A gun or knife was too violent and not in my character. The thought of using either of those weapons was so blatantly distasteful that it turned my stomach, or it might have been the effects of the champagne. A gun was probably out of the question anyway because we didn't have any firearms, and acquiring one would be complicated and unrealistic, let alone learn how to load and shoot a gun well enough to be successful. A knife was easily attainable, but I knew I would never be able to cause enough damage to successfully end my life. I tried cutting myself a few times but never went deep enough to even leave a scar. I got through the first layer of skin, but the pain made me stop abruptly. I never felt the release of freedom or sense of ease others claimed from cutting. The thought of making a cut deep enough to bleed out or stabbing myself deep into my body cavity was too unbecoming of an option.

Jumping from a bridge seemed like it would be easy. Really no planning required—just leap and fly through the air until the crash, preferably into water so there would be double the chance of success with drowning. But what if it didn't work? I've heard of people jumping only to hit something on the way down that *saved* them. I didn't want to be left with devastating injuries, which would lead to an even worse life than I had now. Mom would probably cast me off into an institution, grateful to allow someone else to take care of me.

Hanging. I looked for a downside of this option but could not find one. It would be quick and tidy if done correctly. No one would interrupt me because no one paid attention to me. There would not be anyone to stumble across me and potentially *save* me if it was done in the right place. It fit my persona, since I drifted through this life trying to find my place and I would drift my way into the afterlife. There were few external factors that could change the outcome. I would be completely in control, and it would hold enough shock value to achieve the recognition I desired.

How long would it be until I would be discovered? Days? Weeks? Would it only be after the unpleasant smell had someone searching for its origin? My nausea returned, and I sprinted to the bathroom just in time to empty my stomach of the brunch and champagne.

WORTHLESS

I slept restlessly that night. I kept having strange snippets of broken dreams. A dark hallway. Eerie fog. A tipped-over chair. A note crumbled on the floor, collecting dust. I woke up the next morning with lingering notions of suicide and seriously started to contemplate if it could or should be the answer. My thoughts were consumed by the logistics.

To entertain it as an actual possibility, I needed to do research. I prided myself in thorough, well-thought-out ideas, and now that I decided hanging would be the best mode for success, I had a new obsession. I poured over the internet and found all the answers I needed to create a foolproof plan—it had everything I wanted to know about noose types, best materials, and knot tying. Soon I found myself in the corner hardware store perusing the aisles for the items I needed. Once, a store clerk startled me as I was tugging on a section of braided leather. I broke into a sweat, concocting an impromptu story about trying to make my own horse reins, and I quickly exited the store. I chose a new store and made my visits shorter to avoid any suspicion and questions. I wound up ordering most of the things I needed online, since it seemed the best way to limit any potential hindrance.

Location. Where should I hang myself? I wanted it to be memorable as my last act on earth but needed to weigh the importance of not being discovered too early as well. The high school was an option. Since I had been trying relentlessly to make myself recognized there, it would have a poetic justice sort of feel to it, and yet it didn't feel quite right. I also would have a high probability of being found before the deed was done. The bridge leading out of town? It would be like a last farewell to the town and my life. That, too, had many risks of failure, as people might stop and intervene before I was successful. My house? This seemed like the best option. It would allow the act to be under my control without outside influences, and my mom was not likely to be around to cause a problem. But where in the house? What spot would provide the best possibility for success and be strong enough to hold my weight?

I walked around the house, examining each room with fresh eyes, and imagining a noose hanging from various positions. As I went through the kitchen, living room, bathrooms, and bedrooms, none seemed suitable, and all would have had the same risk of Mom interrupting the moment by coming home unexpectedly. My thoughts drifted to the attic and how my mom had been so horrified to find me spending time there. I had always intended to go back up there to see what had made her so anxious. This seemed like the perfect opportunity to find that out and to gauge if the conditions were right for what I wanted to do.

On a Friday morning, I waited for Mom to leave for work. She was talking on her phone while juggling her coffee and designer bag and rushing out the door. As usual, she didn't say goodbye. I instantly went to the attic door and found it still locked. Mom wasn't kidding that she didn't want me in there. A quick YouTube tutorial allowed me to easily open the old-fashioned lock without even damaging the door jamb. The door opened with a loud creaking, echoing through the hallway. The stale smell of dust and musty old boxes hit me like the perfume of a freshly sprayed skunk and made me hesitate before entering.

INTRIGUE

———

I ventured past the cobwebs to feel along the edge of the wall for a light switch, but I couldn't find one. When I had relocated to the attic awhile back, I never really explored the space. I simply chose to camp out in a corner of the room, making a fort with blankets. I never even tried to find a light, content to use a flashlight at the time. But now I needed to know what was in here, so I grabbed my cell phone from my pocket to use the flashlight and found the overhead pull chain for a single lightbulb.

The light intensified as the bulb warmed up and started to cast shadows across piles of haphazard boxes, totes, and furniture. In a corner, some of the blankets I used to make my fort were still hanging in place, heavy with time and dust. I was astounded to get my first good look at the rest of the attic. It looked like a whole other life was stashed here. I had never seen Mom take anything in or out of the attic and couldn't imagine where all this stuff had come from.

I started with the box closest to me. I opened it up and found folded women's clothes—sweatshirts, T-shirts with old slogans, a pair of plaid pants. Must be some of Mom's old wardrobe items from her younger days. I pushed it aside and reached for another box. It also contained old clothes, as did the next box and the box after that. Why did Mom keep all of this stuff? It wasn't like she would ever wear any of it again, as focused as she was on buying the latest fashions that hit the stores. I moved the boxes aside so that I could reach a stack of totes. I stubbed my toe as I maneuvered around the corner of a desk and screamed more in shock than from pain. I reached down to rub it and caught a glimpse of photos in the desk's partially opened bottom drawer. I yanked the drawer open, as it was a little bit stuck, and found a stack of framed photos of someone I didn't recognize. A woman who had a resemblance to Mom, but definitely was not her.

For some reason that I couldn't explain, I felt a strong connection to this woman and sense of solidarity. There were about a dozen framed photos in the drawer, but there weren't any names written on the back. I opened the rest of the drawers, looking for clues about this mystery woman. Much to my disappointment, I couldn't find anything. I tore through some of the nearby totes and boxes but was unable to link anything else to the woman. If the photos were important enough to keep, why didn't I know who she was? If she wasn't important, why not get rid of the photos?

I must have lost track of time, as I heard the garage door opening, meaning that Mom was home. I didn't want to risk her finding me in the attic and freaking out again, especially since I had found something intriguing and wanted more time to figure it out. I hastily put things back in order, grabbed one of the photos, and snapped the light off. I hustled out of the attic, locked the door again, and went to my room. I stashed the photo in my own desk drawer, feeling guilty as if I had stolen something from a store but also experiencing a sense of hidden promise.

RESOLUTE

I returned to the attic every day for two weeks, searched every nook and cranny, but was unable to find even the faintest clue to the identity of the woman. Mark it down as another failure. With this setback and a renewed feeling that my days had no purpose, my depression came roaring back with a vengeance. I took to skipping meals again, as I had no appetite and felt a constant sourness in my stomach. My shower developed a layer of dusty, moldy-smelling scum on the bottom, as I had stopped bathing. My room was a catastrophe, with dirty and random piles of stuff thrown everywhere. I spent entire days locked in my bedroom again, lying in bed for hours at a time without any movement or organized line of thinking.

Just a vast desert of emptiness.

Almost as if I had already died.

Complete and utter nothingness.

Catatonia.

As I lay there, trying to will myself into forming any cohesive thoughts, I realized my failed search of the attic had at least one useful purpose. I finally found the perfect location for me to move forward with my suicide plans, if I could get motivated enough to take action. Since I had done a lot of grunt work by moving aside boxes while I was looking for the identity of the mystery woman, I had created the perfect spot for hanging myself without even intending to do so. There was a beam along the outside wall that could definitely hold my weight, I would be able to navigate the height to get my noose positioned correctly and would have enough clearance that there would not be an error. There was even a little crack in the roofline where light shone through and, at just the right time of day, passed over the spot. I put a chair in this spot during the last couple weeks while I was sorting through boxes. A sense of peace overcame me in the stillness while I observed the glimmers of dust in the beams of sunlight. Such calm in the chaos of the attic. I only hoped I could experience this calm mindset during my last moments of life, which would occur in just a few short days if my plans came to fruition.

I was just waiting for one final delivery of the last necessary component, scheduled for the next day, and then my orchestrated plan could be implemented. The last few days had solidified my intent to move forward, as I had nothing but time to lie on the floor, thinking of how life was passing by without me. I kept running scenarios through my head that might make me change my mind by finding meaning in my life, but I came up short. I thought through the last several months and remembered nothing but pain, exclusion, despair, fear, and worthlessness. As I contemplated the final steps of my preparations, I became more resolved in believing that suicide was the best solution. I saw no point in my continued presence on this earth and was determined to create a memorable farewell. I was insistent that I would establish a name for myself by my dramatic departure and absence and, more importantly, it would justify my angst all along.

Musing about how the final pieces were coming together gave me a boost of energy, and I raised myself from the floor. I needed everything to go as planned, and for that, I needed to focus on every detail as I would not tolerate yet another failure. By successfully planning and completing my suicide, I could finally conquer something in my life. My most important achievement to date.

Thursday would be the day.

Thursday, I would make my final statement and hang myself.

GOODBYE

Dear Mom,

I wonder how long it took you to find this note. You never noticed anything about me or my life. Why should my death be that much different? I tried and tried, and this world rejected me every step of the way, so I am leaving it behind and getting the upper hand on it for just this once.

~your unseen daughter

I left the note on my pillow. This was it. I went to the attic and took in the scene before me. My initial unintentional chair placement had been perfected to align with the angle of the sun streaming through the small slit in the roof, waiting to cascade the brilliance of the suspended dust particles in the air. My noose tied to perfection, with triple-checked knots, was hanging above the chair over the strongest part of the beam, confirmed by my testing earlier in the week.

There was a transcendent moment of silence as I stepped onto the chair and tested the strength of the rope for one last time and waited for the light to come through the crack— just enough time for me to take a deep, cleansing, calming breath. I wanted it to be quick, and I wanted to make sure I left on my own terms without mistakes. I loosened the rope to slip my head inside, feeling the weight of the rope on my shoulders. I started to tighten the knot, and then I heard the doorbell ring.

All I could think was that my one victory in life was going to be ruined; I couldn't even determine the timing of my own death. At first, I ignored the bell; nothing was going to change my mind. But the damn doorbell kept on ringing, and then the person started banging on the door. I couldn't take it. This was not my plan, but plans must be adapted to make them perfect. I would try again tomorrow to achieve perfection, for it had to be just as I planned. It had to be on my terms to make it matter.

I loosened the noose and took my head out, feeling the weight lift from my shoulders. I made my way downstairs and answered the door. There was a girl standing there with her face all red and scrunched up from pounding and yelling. She was holding a piece of cardboard or something. She just stood and stared. How annoying! My attempt spoiled for this?

Just as I was shutting the door, she blurted out, "Are you Marissa Adams? Did you draw this?"

She turned the piece of cardboard around. It was one of my drawings from an art class I had taken last semester. Why would she have this? It was an abstract drawing of the many twists and turns a person's life could take as they try to weave their own cloth. I really enjoyed this piece and thought it depicted my inner mind quite appropriately. I looked away from the drawing, managed to nod yes, and shut the door. I leaned back against the cool, solid surface of the door, ignoring her continued questions and knocks. I took a deep breath, started to shake soundlessly, and then dissolved into hysterics. Somebody actually took time from their day to find me—me! And she brought me the one piece of art that spoke to my current state of mind. Each pathway had a different set of turns, but all arrived at the same state of happiness and completeness at their ending.

"I am Marissa Adams. I AM Marissa Adams. I am MARISSA ADAMS, and this is MY LIFE."

My life; not my death. Mine.

DISGUST

Now what? My mind was stuck on the image of me standing on the edge of the chair, toes just creeping past the edge with the weight of the rope on my neck, and the scratch of the rope on my skin. Ten seconds. Ten seconds was what stood between my life and my death. Timing was instrumental in me sitting here on the floor, alive. But why? Why did it turn out this way? Was there a bigger reason why I should be alive? The shuddering realization of what almost happened scared me. As I sat with a million questions, I came to one conclusion. I realized suicide was a selfish delusion. How childish to think my death would make my life worth any more than it was while I was living it. It would mark me as more selfish and despicable than everything I had stood against over the last couple of months. How could I possibly think it would be my way of making a lasting impression? How conceited. But, seriously, now what? How did I go forward from this point?

First thing that was a must, I absolutely needed to remove the temptation of suicide again. I rushed to the attic, gathered all my supplies, and threw them in the trash can that was already at the curb for collection. Next, I ran to my room and grabbed the note I had left for my mom and used the candle from my desk to burn it in the bathroom sink.

As the last wafts of smoke dissipated in the air, I expelled a breath that I didn't realize I was holding. That took care of the immediate threat of another suicide attempt. Gathering all the right materials again would take time, and if I got to that point, hopefully time would serve as a buffer and safeguard me from entertaining any such thoughts for long. I knew there was a possibility that my depression might worsen, and I had to protect myself from believing that suicide was the right answer.

How could I prevent myself from considering suicide again? I did a simple internet search and was so overwhelmed that I slammed my laptop shut. There were lifelines and websites and videos, but for some reason, I couldn't stomach clicking on a single link. I guess I was afraid of labeling myself as a suicide risk, though that's clearly what I was. The very act of trying to get help created a barrier to moving forward with any sort of action step. No wonder so many people stayed sullen and lost within the demons of their minds.

I waited until I heard Mom come home from work and disappear into her room to change clothes. I made my way down the hallway to her door and stood hesitantly outside, my hand suspended to knock, but instead I backed away. I couldn't remember the last real conversation I had had with her. How could I even begin this one? Fear overcame my desire to ask her for help. She would probably dismiss me just like she had every other time I had attempted to get her attention and thus reinforce the worthlessness I was already feeling. The sensation of being lost returned, and I began to spiral. I don't remember leaving the hallway, but I woke up in my bed several hours later, disoriented by the darkness of the night and disillusioned by the crucial events of today. Was it even still today? One look at my phone confirmed that yes, indeed, it was still the same day. My mind and body felt complete exhaustion. I pulled the blankets over my head, trying to will myself to go back to sleep. I was blindly hoping for a miracle that when I awoke the answers would be clear-cut and I would find a hint of a way out of this mess.

TRAPPED

No such luck. I was stuck in limbo. I knew I did not want to commit suicide and was now at least temporarily certain I would never attempt again, but I was just as miserable as always. I was rejected by my peers at school, unable to talk to my mom, and without any purpose or direction to my life. Who would even see me when I couldn't even see myself? The girl who had come to my house seemed to know of me or at least my artwork, but I didn't even know her name. I thought I should find out who she was. She saved my life. Literally. Without her incessant ringing of the doorbell and knocking, I would have acted on my plan.

That was what I could start with—a quest to find this girl. I knew she must go to my school because she had my artwork. As the former queen of gossip, how was it possible that I didn't know who she was or have even a glimmer of recognition? Maybe she was a new student who had arrived after I gave up my desire to track the ins and outs of everyone else. I used some of my old tactics to try and figure out who this mystery girl was, hanging out by the lockers and the girls' bathroom, but to my dismay, I could not determine her identity. I was really frustrated by how far my skills had slipped. This was my wheelhouse, and I was failing.

Then it dawned on me. She had my artwork that I did on the theme of feeling lost in the sea of life and the difficulty of figuring out who you are and how to follow your own path. Something I had incessantly searched for but had not yet found. She might be feeling just as lost as I was. I always thought this feeling was unique to me. Everyone else seemed to have it all figured out. Could there actually be another girl in school who felt the same things I was feeling and was desperately hoping to find another person who could relate? My hopes rose for the first time in what felt like a lifetime, and I actually felt a glimmer of lightness in my chest.

The next morning, I went to the creative arts wing of the high school, nearly sprinting, eager to meet the girl who had knocked on my door. I dashed into each of the classrooms but did not recognize her in the array of faces staring back at me. I was out of breath by the time I reached the end of the hallway. I nearly broke down outside the last door, as I was certain that I would not be able to find her. I was failing yet again in a mission that seemed like my only hope. Why couldn't I ever do anything right? The familiar self-doubt and despair started to set in when the teacher, Ms. Clayton, reached out and touched my arm. I jumped back, startled. She smiled. "Marissa, you look scared. What can I help you with?" How did she know my name? I stared at her and realized she was my teacher when I did that pivotal art piece in question. I remembered I had always liked her.

I tried to explain that I was looking for a student, but all I could get out was a stuttering mess of words. She squeezed my arm slightly and directed me to stay in the hallway as she turned back toward her classroom and gave her students directions to start their projects. I wouldn't have been able to move, even if I tried. I was frozen in place.

Ms. Clayton turned back to me and, with the greatest kindness I had ever experienced, led me down the hallway to an alcove where we could sit together and have a private conversation. She looked me in the eye and said, "Whatever it is, I can help you." I stared back at her, not sure if I heard her correctly, and wondered if I could trust her. I held her gaze for what seemed like hours but in reality was only a minute or two. I took a few deep breaths and blurted out that I was trying to find a student, whom I quickly described, so I could talk to her and thank her because she is the only reason for me to have any hope in this life.

The last bit slipped out unintentionally. I panicked. I wasn't supposed to tell her my secret. I immediately looked up, returning Ms. Clayton's gaze. I expected to see anger, pity, or dismissal, but instead all I saw was warmth and understanding. Even more importantly, she didn't go into the soothing mode of saying "everything will be okay, it can't be that bad, it's just a rough patch" or the many other platitudes I had heard dished out over the years. She seemed genuinely concerned—at least enough for me to gather my composure and continue a conversation. She let me talk, and honestly to this day, I am unsure what I rambled on about or how much I revealed.

The next thing I remembered was sitting in the school nurse's office. How I arrived there, I was not quite certain, but I clearly recalled sitting at the edge of the couch, digging my fingernails into the rigid, commercial-grade cushions, trying to maintain a grip on something concrete so I wouldn't lose it. Ms. Clayton must have brought me here. I heard whispers outside the door, and my sense of panic returned. They must be talking about me, I thought, and I sat in fear about what might be coming next. I thought about trying to leave, but there was no way to escape with so many people standing right outside the door. Beads of sweat started down my back, my breathing quickened, my hands shook as I awaited the unknown. This was torture.

SHAME

The door opened, and I saw a sea of faces that all seemed to blur into one. How could Ms. Clayton do this to me? I trusted her!! Shame overtook me, and I found myself trying to melt into the couch, longing to disappear. I was finally being seen, but this was far from the original plan. They didn't see me as me; they saw a problem that needed to be handled.

I heard a voice break through the crowd. "Marissa, Marissa, do you hear me? Stop staring off. Look at me. Marissa!" I blinked a few times and looked up into the face of the person who was speaking—none other than my mother. My mom! At school! This was a first. I was so astounded that I just stared at her and could not form any words. She had made it clear that she did not want to be disturbed at work, and yet here she stood in front of me. She pushed her way through everyone else and slammed the door behind her.

The shock of it all sent a shiver through my spine and then brought me back to the moment, snapping me out of an imminent panic attack. She did not make any sound or movement at first and just looked at me. I bowed my head and started to feel hot tears on my face because I knew she was disappointed and would be mortified that our perfect family appearance had been shattered wide open. I tried to think of an excuse to pass the blame and say that it was a misunderstanding, but she closed the distance between us and wrapped me in a hug. It was awkward at first because I could not recall the last time I felt her embrace, but she continued to hold me tight, and I relaxed into her arms. I started to speak, but she responded with, "Not now, not here. Let's get home."

Thankful to escape, I nodded my head, as that was all the strength I could muster. She pulled me up from the couch and opened the door, pushed our way past everyone, and escorted me to the car. I experienced such a protective, motherly love with this act and looked at her with new eyes. She was my hero.

We arrived home, and I tried to bolt to my room, but she intercepted me and led me to the dining room table instead. She made tea for us both, adding honey and vanilla, and set the cups on the table. She took her seat next to me and reached for my hand. I instinctively pulled away, but then stopped and returned my hand into hers. I looked up, and her eyes held my gaze. Both of us started crying, and we sat like this for the longest time, long enough for our tea to grow cold and for me to feel the magnitude of this moment. Our relationship was taking a pivotal turn right here and now. I knew more than anything that I couldn't fail at this one; we had to figure it out.

We didn't talk about what happened in the nurse's office, we didn't talk about my confessions to Ms. Clayton. I didn't know what the school had told Mom to prompt her arrival, and she wasn't letting on about that either. It didn't seem to matter at the time. All Mom cared about was maintaining the physical bond of our hands, and she told me how much she loved me. She stroked my hair away from my face, and she assured me that she was there for me. I sobbed and sobbed until I ran out of tears and felt empty all the way through to my bones. The desperation in which I longed for these words dulled in comparison to finally experiencing them.

HESITANT

The next morning, I opened my eyes to my mom sitting on the edge of my bed, still wearing pajamas, hair not done, makeup not completed, and holding her morning coffee. I blinked a few times, not remembering the last time I saw Mom look so relaxed and frankly like a mom instead of a career-centered woman done to perfection. I smiled slightly and sat up in bed. She put her hand on my arm and told me that we were taking the day off together. No work, no school. Just a day for us at home. I stared back at her. This had never happened, and I didn't know how to respond. My silence did not discourage her, and she assured me it would be a very important day to spend together and to hit the reset button on life.

She guided me out of bed and coaxed me downstairs. I followed her as if in a dream state until I found myself seated at the kitchen island with breakfast in front of me—a plate piled high with French toast, scrambled eggs, and bacon with a cup of special coffee. I could not recall her ever making breakfast like this. She settled herself next to me with her own plate, and while she barely touched her food, I devoured mine. It was delicious. I let out a sigh, and Mom smiled at me. She took a deep breath, smoothed her hair behind her ear, pursed her lips together slightly, opened her mouth to speak, and then closed it. Clearly, she had no idea what to say.

I cut her some slack. This was awkward. We had never done this before. The very fact that she had reached out this much was commendable, and rather than be annoyed, I started to feel empathy for her. She looked just as lost as I was. How could two people living under the same roof have so much space between them?

I broke the silence. "Mom, thank you for coming to school yesterday. I didn't know how much I needed you until I saw you in the nurse's office."

Her lips trembled, her face turned blotchy, she started to shake ever so slightly, and she started to cry. At first, just a few tears escaped with a trail down her cheek, and then she dissolved into all-out sobbing. She pulled me in close to her, wrapping her arms around me like a mama bear corralling her cubs, and I could feel the love pour out of her. "Were you really happy to see me?" She was looking for just as much reassurance as I was.

STUNNED

I needed a moment and some distance from Mom. This was a lot, all at once, when for so long there had been nothing. I excused myself to take a shower, hoping this was a plausible enough reason to step away without hurting her feelings. I let the hot water stream down my back while I tried to collect my thoughts and find the strength for a long day of emotional outpouring. I turned the faucet off, and the dripping of the water, the gurgle of the drain, and the whirring of the exhaust fan created a background symphony to my daze. The cold air hit me, returning me to the present, and I exhaled hard, trying to expel any feelings of fear and worthlessness from my mind and body.

I wanted to continue talking to Mom, but I feared where the conversation would go next. I was not ready to talk about the depth of my depression, my thoughts of suicide, let alone my nearly successful attempt. I got up the nerve to head back downstairs and found the living room empty; I relaxed instantly, feeling my shoulders drop away from my ears and my breaths become a little easier. I snuggled on the sofa with the plush pillows and well-worn quilt and felt safe. Safe from myself, safe from the outside world, and safe from whatever the day may hold. I was starting to drift back to sleep when Mom entered the room. She sat on the couch, holding a framed photo, the tension in her body increasing as she inched closer to me.

"This is your Aunt Holly."

Reflexively, I gasped as I immediately recognized the person in the photo to be the same woman in the photo hidden in my desk upstairs. The answer I had eagerly searched for was lying within my mom's memories this entire time. She stared wistfully at the picture as she went on. "She was my younger sister. She was full of life, full of independence, and full of pain that I never saw until it was too late."

The revelation took a moment for me to comprehend, and when I did, I met my mom's eyes. She just nodded, before clamping her eyes closed, the weight of her pain bowing her head low. I felt hot tears forming at the corners of my eyes. Since when had I become so weepy?

She went on to tell me about how Holly struggled through high school with being the outsider of every group. When she was in college, she seemed to discover herself. She stepped into the life she had always sought, but her old self-destructive demons came back after she didn't get into a popular sorority house with the rest of her friends. Her devastation triggered her depression, and her mental well-being suffered tremendously. She couldn't cope and started drinking alcohol heavily and dabbling with drugs. She slipped into a silent depression that she covered up with excuses of being preoccupied with her classes and effectively hid it all from her family by distancing herself at college—not coming home for weekend visits, not returning phone calls, missing family birthday dinners. Rather than being seen as a sign she needed help, she was praised for being so dedicated to her studies.

Mom said everyone was in shock when Holly killed herself because no one anticipated it as Holly had covered her depression and substance abuse up so well, and her family split apart as a result. No one could bear the pain and being together only caused a deeper divide as they tried to ignore the unspeakable hurt of her death. They all felt responsible and could not forgive themselves, casting the blame on each other rather than coping with her death properly.

"How could I not even know about her or that you even had a sister?" I asked in astonishment.

The expression on Mom's face stopped me cold from asking a string of lamenting questions that were forming in my brain.

"It was easier for me at the time to pretend she never existed than looking at her face every day and knowing I had failed her," she said. "I should have recognized some sign of her depression. Her pulling away, her distance, her silence itself should have raised an alarm. We used to be so close, and her avoidance hurt me deeply at the time, but I thought our bond would return once she finished school and wasn't preoccupied by college life. Afterwards, I felt like such a fool. I should have intervened before it was too late. I should have been the one to save her. I live with guilt every day. Having her pictures out or talking about her only intensified my shame and hurt."

All I could do was stare at Mom. I wasn't sad, I wasn't mad. I'm not sure what I felt. I was completely numb with this new information. I was not prepared for this revelation. I sat in shock, not knowing how to proceed.

Now the attic made complete sense. All the boxed possessions I had sorted through that didn't seem to fit Mom's personality or interests actually belonged to Holly. Her entire life shoved into a small space to be ignored, forgotten, as if she never existed in this world. My irritation rose. How dare she try to erase her memory! But if Mom really wanted it gone, why not get rid of everything to make it easier on herself? These two conflicting views didn't mesh, and I wondered what Mom was really feeling. She may not have even known herself.

"When the principal called me to school yesterday, I was in disbelief," Mom admitted. "How could I have history repeat itself right under my nose and not see it for the second time? I rushed to the school praying I wasn't too late and that I would be able to make a difference this time. I couldn't stand the thought that my own daughter was headed in the same direction as Holly."

I continued to blankly stare at her, feeling a coldness deep within me return. Did she want to truly help me, or was her concern out of her own self-interests? Could she not bear to have her guilt expanded to encompass two lives that she would need to pretend didn't exist? Even with her sister's death, Mom still made it all about her. How she failed, how she couldn't bear to look at her sister's pictures or belongings. But what about Holly and her memory? The shudder crept down my spine slowly at first and then built in intensity, nearly knocking me off my place on the couch.

Years with my mom had taught me that she always, always put appearances first. She played her part perfectly. Was she trying to fool me with this appearance of concern so that she could ease her guilty conscience? Was the need for conveying a perfect appearance developed after the loss of Holly, or was it something inherent within her? Maybe all these years she had created her own charade as a cover for her own depression and a veil for hiding her true fears. Either way, my mind was whirling, and my world was turned upside down. I tasted a rising sourness in my mouth and felt cold sweat on my neck, pressure in my chest, and a flush of heat in my face. I dashed up the stairs two at a time, and I made it to the bathroom just in time.

CONFUSED

Mom came upstairs and placed a cool compress on my neck as I continued to lie on the bathroom floor. I was so confused and adrift, but it was a completely different kind of lost than from weeks ago. My thoughts were swimming with new information, trying to make sense of the revelations of the day, starting with one concrete truth: I had an aunt who seemed just like me, at least in terms of mental health, and I would never have the chance to know her. Forlorn despair pressed into me, and I vowed to go back through the attic with fresh eyes, trying to absorb who Holly was, taking my time intentionally with each item and hoping that trying to know her would help me know myself. The thought of going to the attic where I nearly took my own life was overwhelming, but I clung to the promise and hope the attic might contain.

Mom interrupted my thoughts. "Marissa, I know this has been a lot to process today, but these are the first steps we need to take. We need to have conversations and be able to share the hard stuff. I thought if I shared some of my past with you so that you would realize that I have experience with it, you might be able to start sharing what has been going on with you."

I wanted to believe that Mom was speaking out of concern for me, but how could I trust she was being sincere? Doubt lingered. She could not be the only one I talked to about this. I must have someone else to be an outside party without a vested interest. I didn't want to slam the door that was opened today, so I took the best approach I knew how.

"Mom, I am going to need more help than just you. I need to talk to someone else who doesn't live with me so that I can feel like my privacy is protected and I can live without feeling like I am constantly under scrutiny. We are brand new at this, and there is a lot I don't want to share with you right now."

She accepted that easier than I expected, and it actually looked like she relaxed a little bit too. Maybe she feared having to be accountable for me being mentally okay. Maybe the weight of her guilt over Holly had damaged her deeper than I had realized, which might explain her distance from me as a mother. Or maybe it was a relief that she could pass the responsibility for my mental health onto someone else, and I was just an obligation that needed to be managed like one of her tasks at work. It was like two edges of a sword, equally sharp, and I still wasn't sure which edge held the truth.

The only thing Mom insisted on knowing that day was if I was safe at home. It struck me like a lightning bolt because just a few days ago, I was not. Now I could confidently tell her I was safe at home but not safe from my own thoughts. That was all I was willing to divulge. I could not cross the bridge into full disclosure until I knew her driving motivation.

SELF-CONSCIOUS

Mom wasted no time. She called multiple offices and questioned staff about the counselors' specialties and credentials before securing an appointment with someone she felt would be a good fit. I was pretty upset because she was acting as if she knew what was best for me from the mere two days she had shown up as a mother. I relented on going to the appointment only after she pleaded with me that morning, telling me how she had called in a special favor to get an appointment with a counselor who was otherwise booked. Since she went to so much trouble, I decided to go. In a way, I was relieved because I hadn't even attempted to find help after being overwhelmed with my first internet search.

I stood on the sidewalk outside the office and tried not to let anger cloud my impressions. The office was more welcoming than I expected. The scent of wildflowers blowing in the warm spring breeze along with the soft wall colors in the reception area allowed me to let my guard down ever so slightly as I took the brave first steps into my first therapy appointment. I thought it would smell of sterility and crispness like a dentist's office, which would have put me on guard with the expectation that the appointment was going to be dreadful. But this felt different. I was able to pull from my brain a peaceful memory that I didn't even know existed. Thankfully, I waited only a few moments before my turn and didn't have to avoid eye contact with anyone or pretend to be interested in the magazines in the waiting room.

Soon I was face to face with a kindly woman, my therapist, who started our session with a lengthy monologue. "Hi Marissa. My name is Dr. Prescott. I'm glad you were able to come in today. Since this is new to you, I wanted to let you know a few things before we get started. Everything we discuss during our sessions is strictly confidential. I will not disclose any of our conversations to your mother or anyone else. I am here to help you, but it will require work from you as well. I am here as your guide as you start to navigate your way through your emotions, thoughts, impressions, and any questions you'd like to ask. Some days you might get mad at me because I might push an issue that strikes a personal chord, or I might bring up painful memories or tackle sensitive subjects. These are important milestones in your therapy, even though they run the risk of making you feel like you want to give up. Those are the most crucial times for you to lean in and trust me and my expertise. Do you understand and agree to put forth the effort?"

I won't lie. I was a little dumbfounded. I thought she would just preach at me about how life was worth living, that I had my mind twisted by backwards notions from society, and it was on me to figure out how to make myself okay. This was better. She was encouraging me to be an active participant and express my thoughts instead of just listening to her expert solutions. She seemed to know what she was talking about, and I definitely thought it was worth giving her a shot.

"Yes, I understand."

"Good, then let's get started. I want you to push yourself headfirst into these beginning exercises so that we can get a base of familiarity and do away with small talk to make our sessions more effective. This is not the time to skirt the real answers, give half-truths, or pretend to answer how you think I want you to. That would be a waste of both my time and yours."

She meant business. Yet, oddly, it was a relief. I needed the structure, the direction, the task-oriented focus. I laid the first bomb on her, "I have been using alcohol to help cope and need help stopping that too," ducking my head into my sweatshirt collar and waiting for a lecture.

Dr. Prescott didn't shake her head in shame, didn't tsk-tsk with her tongue, didn't react at all how I expected. She merely looked me in the eye and said, "Okay, thank you for the honesty. We will get to that. Any other substances or risky behaviors that we need to address?"

We. She said we. I wouldn't have to have all the answers or figure out the next steps by myself.

I was not alone.

INEPT

The first few steps onto the street after my appointment made me feel like a new person. I saw the bright colors of the fresh flowers outside the market, smelled the aroma of freshly baked bread in the bakery, and heard the laughter of young kids as they entered the ice cream shop, eagerly discussing which flavor they would get today. Everything seemed more alive. I inhaled a deep breath and smiled. How could I have missed all of this over the last year? How could I be surrounded by so much life and not take notice of the simple joys?

Then it happened. I saw Tyler walking down the street toward me, and I immediately panicked. What if he saw me come out of my psychiatrist's office? I quickly tried to have an excuse ready, to hide my embarrassment, but it proved unnecessary. He walked right past me, no eye contact, no moving over slightly to give me extra room, no acknowledgement of my presence at all. I could have jumped up and down, made faces, and he probably still would have ignored me. Ignored, yet again. My fleeting moment of happiness was spoiled. I knew it was too good to be true. My appointment had made me forget the reality of my life.

I headed home and found Mom, making dinner and eager to hear about my appointment.

"How did it go? Is she nice? Did you like her? Is this going to work?"

She didn't even let me answer one question before going on to the next one. I was overwhelmed and still feeling shunned by the encounter with Tyler. My face must have told the story because Mom dropped the questions. She dished up some dinner on my plate, and told me to sit down and eat. She seemed disappointed, but I didn't have the energy or the desire to tell her it was actually Tyler who had made me so sullen and not the therapy session. I managed to eat a few bites and then excused myself from the table.

Staring out the window while sitting at my desk, I replayed the afternoon. I felt good. Scratch that. I felt great. I didn't even know I could feel like that anymore. It was such an odd sensation, but it was even better than when I was on the dance floor surrounded by my peers. *It was something from within me that didn't rely on anyone else.* Dr. Prescott really seemed to understand me, and I knew it sounded stupid to think after just one session I could have such hope, but I did. I needed to. I didn't have any other direction to head. Experiencing Tyler's continued rejection hurt a lot, more than I wanted it to, but I didn't know how to change my need for approval and inclusion. How could I make my desire to fit in disappear?

I looked at the book Dr. Prescott sent home with me, which contained the exercises I was supposed to work on before our next session. I couldn't bring myself to open it. What if I failed at this too? What if it asked things I couldn't admit to myself, let alone talk about with someone else? Damn, this was going to be awful. She warned me about this, though, and said the more I worked on the exercises, the easier they would get. The first couple were always the most difficult, and she said it would take an immense amount of courage to start. The faith she had in me was just like a mother bird kicking the baby bird out of the nest for the first time, knowing its wings would have the strength to fly. I had my own hesitations about the process, but I had committed to her to put in the work, and I don't go back on my word. She challenged me to look deep within myself and not allow external factors to affect my every move. I repeated my new mantra to myself—*You are strong, you are brave, and you can do hard things*—and opened the book.

The first page was an "About Me" section, which was broken it into different bullet points that I needed to complete about my appearance, my talents, my goals, and my fears. I filled in some of them without giving them much thought. I re-read them afterwards and realized they could describe a multitude of people and didn't necessarily pertain to just me. I added more details in the margins and tried to provide a description that would give Dr. Prescott a semblance of who I was. I wanted her to like me. Again, here I was expressing a need for approval. This was a recurring theme, and I realized how much my inner turmoil had been caused by it. I put it into the fear section.

The next page asked about my family. It had always been just my mom and me. My dad was never in the picture, and according to Mom, we were better off that way. I wasn't even sure if he was alive. We never went to extended family gatherings, and until this week, I never understood why. Holly. My knowledge of my family was so limited and incomplete. I had many more questions than answers. I couldn't bring myself to complete anything on that page and closed the workbook. Every forward step seemed to be followed by three or four backwards steps, ready to drag me back into the darkness.

SHY

My mom let me stay out of school for two weeks on the psychiatrist's recommendation, and I was beyond thankful for this small grace. She seemed to do whatever Dr. Prescott suggested, and if I'm being fair, Mom had been beyond understanding. All the things I always thought moms should do were slipping into the rhythm of our days. Cookbooks, recipes printed out from the computer, and shopping lists were scattered across the counter now instead of the stack of take-out menus we usually picked from. There were little things Mom did that made me know she was working on changing. Checking in on me before bed, asking about the high and low of my day (this was one of the exercises Dr. Prescott asked us to do to help us connect, and honestly, it was working). Watching a movie with me instead of flitting off somewhere with her friends at night. Texting me during her lunch breaks at work. While I always assumed, or hoped, Mom had love for me in her own way, I no longer questioned it. I solidly believed she had my best interests at heart and would help me however I asked.

My first day back at school was interesting. It felt like I was a new kid in school. People held my gaze as I walked down the hallways and tipped their heads in casual greeting. No one talked to me still, but at least they saw me. For real, saw me. I had strived for this moment for so many months that it was a little unnerving, making me look over my shoulder to see who was behind me or feeling an uncomfortable flush come across my face. I was at my locker, and my locker mate said, "Hi." I stuttered a "Hello" back, and my backpack slid down my arm, making me drop my books and make a spectacle of myself, so much so that she looked back in disgust, shook her head, and went off to class. So much for my re-entrance into school.

I attended my morning classes without any changes to previous days, except I did pay more attention to the teacher and ignored the gossip going on around me. Dr. Prescott warned me that I needed to focus on myself and not get distracted when I went back to school or fall into old habits. During study hall, I had nothing to do, so I pretended to go to the bathroom like I had so many times before, but this time I went to the art wing of the high school. I needed to find Ms. Clayton and express my gratitude. I found her helping a student in the back of one of the studios. I felt the same lightness that I sometimes felt in therapy and knew I was on the right track, letting intuition guide me. I tried to wait it out so that I could be alone with her, but there did not seem to be any end to the conversation with the other student, so I politely interrupted.

Ms. Clayton turned to me, and a quick smile washed across her face. She welcomed me with an air of relief. "Marissa, I am so happy to see you back at school. Will you be joining one of my classes again to finish the school year?"

"Wait. You are Marissa?" the other student blurted out.

Shame enveloped me, and I immediately withdrew, backing away to the hallway. Everyone must know about my incident, and now I was the freak who was going to a psychiatrist and couldn't handle being a teenager. I started to spiral again, feeling the blood drain from my face and sweat on my neck begin to form, just like the last time I was in this hallway. At least one of my goals was finally completed, my peers knew of me—albeit as a freak.

"Marissa, no, stay here. You are misunderstanding. This is Julia. Julia came to your house about a month ago with your artwork with my permission."

I stopped dead in my tracks. It was her. The one I had been trying to find. The one I owed my life to. I simply stared back at her, unable to do anything else. My mind was exploding with what I wanted to say, but nothing came out. I panicked more than when I thought she was mocking me just moments before. I fled. Just like when I slammed the door in her face.

RESTLESS

What a chickenshit. I had no words for my cowardice earlier today. What an utter disgrace. I paced my bedroom countless times before my mom swung by to check in and immediately saw me in distress. She tried to talk gently to me, tried the breathing exercises that we had used in the past, tried to smother me in a hug, and I still wasn't able to relax. I screamed. Man, did that catch us both off-guard. My mom acted as if she was shocked by an electrical outlet, but the moment of silence afterwards brought calmness and clarity.

I confessed to Mom what happened at school with Julia, and she suggested I make an extra appointment with Dr. Prescott to talk it over because she feared this would cause regression in my progress, especially since it occurred on my very first day back. That was probably the best instinct she could have had because I didn't know how to help myself, and Mom couldn't do much to help either. Pacing in my bedroom certainly wasn't going to get me any closer to a solution. She called the office and was able to set up a video session for me later that evening. I tried to go through some of the workbook from the previous few sessions, but it seemed pointless to me, and I felt so inadequate that I nearly ripped out the pages in frustration. How could one day offer such optimism and another such hopelessness?

Thankfully, Dr. Prescott knew just how to handle my perceived setback. Instead of focusing on me running away from the art hallway, she focused on everything that went well for the day. How I was able to interact with the person at the locker next to me, how I stayed away from the gossip, that I had the nerve to go and thank Ms. Clayton in the first place. I knew this was her job, but man, I felt empowered and in control again. She bolstered me by encouraging me to focus on the good and not fall back down into the frightening deep trenches of despair. I ended the session feeling like I could at least go back to school the next day.

Mom lurked in the hallway throughout my session. At first, I was incredibly annoyed she was breaking into my usually very private counseling session, but then I relaxed. It's not like we talked about anything I hadn't already told her. Furthermore, it felt awkwardly nice that she was so concerned. Over the last few weeks, Mom had really shown up for me and helped me more in this process than I thought she would. The doubts I held about her trying to shirk her responsibility onto someone else had subsided, and I accepted her intentions as genuine. I opened my door and gave her a big hug.

"Thanks for setting that up, Mom. It was exactly what I needed." She blinked fast, holding back the glimmering tears at the brink of her eyelashes, and she just hugged me tight, allowing her squeeze to say everything required.

MOTIVATED

Okay, school again. I gave myself a pep talk before leaving. Mom tried to convince me to stay home after yesterday's debacle, but I was determined not to hide any longer. I felt confident I would be able to handle myself throughout the day. I donned my two new bracelets before leaving—one from Dr. Prescott and one from my mom. They were meant to invoke strength just by looking at them and were doused with essential oils for good measure. I could do this. *You are strong, you are brave, and you can do hard things.*

I arrived at school early and went straight to Ms. Clayton. She welcomed me into the room just as she had yesterday and graciously accepted my apology for rushing out like a lunatic again. I promised I was trying my hardest but couldn't promise that I wouldn't have more similar episodes.

"It's okay, Marissa. We all struggle with our own inner demons, and how hypocritical would it be of me to hold that against you. I think you should add my class to this semester. You will find space here to explore and create as you evolve into yourself."

I didn't think twice. She was one of the reasons I was succeeding through the last few weeks, and she had led me to getting the help I needed, even though I was so mad at first. I honestly didn't even know what type of art class it was, but I knew I wanted to see her every day. She put me at ease with her presence, and I needed more of that type of energy in my days. It turned out it was a class on photography. Perfect. I found an old camera in the attic that Mom told me was Aunt Holly's, and I was excited to learn how to use it.

I stopped by the guidance counselor's office on my way back down the hall to add the class and adjust my schedule and was immediately hit with a barrage of questions:

"How are you doing?

"How is therapy? Is it working? Did they put you on medication?

"Have you had any more *episodes*? Is that why you are here? Are you going to have one again?"

The wind was knocked out of me like I was sucker-punched. I completely forgot this would, of course, be the same guidance counselor who was one of the faces staring at me after my episode in the art hallway that caused my mom to be summoned. This was exactly the sort of fake concern that had me never wanting to do therapy or talk to anyone at school about my problems. He quashed my excitement just as quickly as it came, but I heard Dr. Prescott's voice in my head and found another solution. I hurriedly left his office and went to the main office instead. The secretary was much kinder. She let me fill out the forms I needed for the class switch and assured me she could take care of the rest and I could start the new schedule tomorrow. I left the office feeling accomplished, feeling strong, and feeling like I was in control.

When Mom got home from work, I was in the kitchen starting on dinner. I felt so empowered and wanted to do something nice for her after putting her through hell the last month. I made some of her favorites—a tossed salad with raspberry vinaigrette, lemon garlic chicken, and rolls I had picked up at the bakery. Mom came through the front door, calling out that she was sorry she was running late and would start dinner in five minutes. She rushed into the kitchen, put her bag down on the desk only to spin around and immediately break into the biggest smile I had ever seen from her. She was utterly glowing and struck speechless. She held her hand clutched to her chest for a moment before rushing over to give me a hug and a blubbering thank-you. I melted into Mom's hug before the oven timer interrupted the moment.

These are the moments I craved in my childhood, and though they were delayed, I was ever so grateful to be experiencing them now. They were becoming less awkward and more natural, but still caught us off-guard in the few seconds afterward when we didn't know how to react to each other. For so long, we had been strangers, merely sharing a house, and now that we were crossing into this new relationship, it was hard to know whether it was more of a friendship or would meld into a standard mother/daughter connection. Through my sessions with Dr. Prescott, she reminded me that we didn't need to label it and should just take each day for what it was. She made it clear to us that our relationship would be unique, and we could morph it into whatever would suit us and not try to force it into a certain category. This reassured both of us that we could navigate as we went and not conform to a standard model or expectation.

INSECURE

I eased into my new routine. My days at school got easier and settled into a predictable pattern, which helped me anticipate the day and mentally prepare. My study halls were now spent in the art wing, and I embraced the new passions that Ms. Clayton helped me discover. I brought in Aunt Holly's camera for Ms. Clayton to look at because it had stumped me, and I could not figure out how to make it work. She examined it with the precision of a surgeon and discovered there was undeveloped film inside that had jammed the back of the camera. She retrieved it without damaging the film, was able to develop it, and the treasures found inside were like looking at a time capsule. Images of my mother emerged in the darkroom, and I couldn't wait to show her these last images that Holly captured. I wanted to preserve the memories for her and bring something good out of the pain she had buried for so long. Ms. Clayton helped put a special protective coating on them so they would last longer and encouraged me to create a nice presentation by putting them in a book.

Ms. Clayton's class was going beautifully until she announced the big partner project. Just hearing her describe it in class made me nauseous. The thought of depending on another person for part of my grade and interacting with someone on a repeated basis made me incredibly uncomfortable and anxious. I went to Ms. Clayton after class and pleaded my case as to why it was a bad idea. She assured me it would be okay; she had intentionally paired me with Julia, thinking we could be good for each other and work well together to complete the project. I still objected and insisted on working by myself even if it would be twice the work, but Ms. Clayton rejected my arguments and said it was required without exception.

Julia and I had our initial meetings during study hall, where we discussed the theme for the project and how we wanted to divide up the work. It was uncomfortable and cumbersome to collaborate like this at first, but we soon settled into a rhythm. Her perspective was a natural complement to my own, and I could see why Ms. Clayton paired us together. We were content to work independently on our designated sections, and our styles melded nicely.

We worked for the next week putting the elements of the project together and ensuring our theme was consistent throughout.

We set a date for an after-school meeting to put on the finishing touches. Since the art rooms were already booked, I suggested that we meet at my house as I needed to feel a sense of security. The last couple of days, I had felt inexplicably on edge and was desperately seeking to keep things on an even keel so that another panic attack would not occur. The night before Julia's visit, I worked on a section of the workbook that Dr. Prescott had provided me. I tried to envision her advice through the exercise, as I needed a bolster of confidence before tomorrow and wanted to abort the weird mindset of the last few days. I couldn't pin down what was bothering me, only that a strange, unsettled feeling had enveloped my thoughts.

The next day, Julia rang the doorbell exactly as scheduled at 4 p.m. Except I didn't hear it. She knocked on the door, and I instantly had a flashback to a memory buried deep in my subconscious from months before when I almost did the unthinkable. I collapsed in the hallway, flushed and panting, and all I could think of was that day—the horror of what I was capable of, the depth of depression I was in, how close I came to completing the act, and the interruption that saved my life. Just like that day, the incessant knocking and ringing of the doorbell eventually pulled me back to the present, and I lifted myself up and staggered my way to the door. I opened the door much like I did months ago, out of breath, annoyed and exasperated to see the very same girl standing there, Julia. The significance of the déjà vu scene before me was engraved into my soul.

Julia rushed her greeting. "Finally! I thought you were never going to answer. I was thinking about how we should present the final picture and the caption, and I think yours might be the stronger statement." She was so wrapped up in the project that she didn't notice my dismayed appearance. I couldn't even form a response but motioned her into the dining room where I had laid out the boards. She immediately went to work, rearranging the last page. I propped myself up against the doorframe and let her have at it because I was still trying to regain my composure while the reel of memories played in my mind.

Julia finally looked up from her work and said, "What is wrong with you? We need to decide on this tonight so we can coordinate the final presentation for next week and get it turned in."

I stared back at her, and all I could do was laugh. At first it was just a soft chuckle, and then it transformed into a full-out belly laugh. I was snorting and laughing so hard that I was crying. I sank to the floor in the doorframe and told her the irony of her showing up months later to again be my savior and friend. She sat down next to me, placed her hands on my hands, and said, "I am here for you, and I want to be your friend. You are important to me, and I need you to be my friend too." I gave her a bear hug, the first one I had ever given, and mumbled, "Thank you."

Julia didn't know exactly what she had saved me from that first day and how significant of a role she played in my life. I wasn't ready to divulge those details to her yet. I felt a pang of guilt for keeping her in the dark, but I couldn't risk losing the only friend I had by telling her the truth and possibly causing her to run scared. For some reason, I was still laughing, and Julia began laughing too. Mom found us giggling on the floor when she got home from work. She just smiled at me and proceeded to the kitchen. She brought us some snacks and then ordered pizza for dinner. Is this what normal feels like?

DEPENDENCE

Alcohol was still exerting control over my life, and it irritated me to no end. I couldn't seem to break my dependence on it. It was like a nice friend saying, "Stay here, you are safe in this zone, you don't want to try and do this without me." I had cut down drastically from what I previously had been drinking but could not let it go completely. I was still relying on it at least three times a week, and that was far too much. I had made such progress with the rest of my therapy, and my days were settling into a better routine than ever before, so I decided it was time to tackle this beast.

Dr. Prescott and I discussed all aspects of why I felt I still needed the alcohol, such as the freedom and ease I associated with it, how it seemed to take the sharp edges of the world away, and the way it made it easier to cope with my anxiety and depression. However, she quickly pointed out that it was a crutch. I had a skewed vision of the benefits alcohol was giving me, and this was a hindrance to delving deeper into my personal issues. It covered the deep layers of my psyche, like a safety net, as if I was afraid of what I might find underneath.

If I wanted to expand beyond the superficial, then breaking away from alcohol was an absolute must. Dr. Prescott reviewed different options available to overcome the addiction. None sounded appealing, but I realized that I was likely incapable of doing it on my own as I had already been trying and failing. I hated to admit that the best chance for success was to do an in-patient rehab program. I didn't know if I could bring myself to do this. It would mean intentionally inserting myself into an unfamiliar setting and experiencing the same type of withdrawal symptoms that had me lying on the kitchen floor not so long ago. I would undoubtedly have panic attacks as a result without my safeguards in place. Willingly submitting to torture—no, thanks.

I voted for a less intensive option that involved going to a group every day—two weeks to start and then gauging if I needed to go longer. It was still in a controlled clinic-type setting with a trained specialist, specifically for adolescent and young adult addiction. This seemed manageable and predictable, which was important to me because I wanted to know what to expect. There was no harm in trying it out, and if it didn't work, I could consider a more intense version or an in-patient detox program. Importantly, it would be after school, so my established routine would not be disrupted, and I would still be able to retreat to my safe zone at home to help control the heightened anxiety and paranoia that comes with withdrawal.

Mom needed to be involved with the decision, which meant confessing to her how much of a problem it was in the first place. I was sure she suspected—she's not stupid—but admitting to her yet another way I had failed was mortifying. Dr. Prescott had arranged for me to start the program the following week, so there was no possibility of delaying the conversation. During dinner, I offered to refill her wine glass, and as I sat back down in my chair, I casually added that I had been finishing her bottles for quite some time as a way to cope with my mental health. She looked at me and simply said, "I know." Of course she knew.

"But Mom, it is worse than you think. I have tried to stop drinking, and I can't. I have become dependent on it and can't go more than two days without having a drink. I know I have to stop, and more importantly, I WANT to stop."

She looked at me and shakily asked, "Do you drink because I am drinking too much? Did you learn this as a coping mechanism from me?"

I had never considered this as why I started and did not think it played a role, so I simply shook my head no. I need not burden her with more guilt and really did not feel it was a contributing factor.

"Mom, I spoke with Dr. Prescott about this already, and she has made arrangements for me to start a program next week to help get me through this next phase of my recovery, if you will sign off on it."

"Of course I will. I want you to succeed in all of your therapy, including substance abuse. Thank you for being honest with me, and if this program doesn't work, we'll find something that will."

Having the conversation behind me was such a relief. Mom took it in stride, probably because she already knew I was drinking even though she hadn't acknowledged it. I wonder what else she knew about and had let me skate by with. Either way, this was progress in our relationship, and I wanted to keep this sort of communication open.

MISERY

Recovery was torture. Scratch that. Withdrawal was torture. Recovery was the phase of your body moving forward after having nothing left to give, but you had to go through hell first to get there. Every single cell of my body was craving alcohol in those first couple of days. I had made it three days on my own in the past before caving into the physical desires and demands of my body because my mind was too weak. I showed up the third afternoon to the clinic as a ghost of myself, shaking, sweating, nauseated, and unable to focus. The counselor gave me a medication tablet, and I simply trusted it would be okay. I didn't even ask questions about what it was or its potential side effects. I was desperate for any of the symptoms to improve.

We continued through the normal session, and I really only heard echoes of voices before Mom picked me up. When we got home, I went straight to bed. All I recall was thrashing around in bed, soaking the sheets, weird segments of dreams, and waking up in a semi-conscious state throughout the night. I missed school on day four, and Mom took me to the session in the afternoon. The counselor gave me the medication again right away, and the combination of both doses seemed to help. I could at least focus on the session a little bit, even though I felt like a blob of flesh on the cold, metal folding chair, willing the stomach cramping to give me a reprieve and the bone-chilling goosebumps to lessen. The counselor assured me over and over that this was a normal part of the detox and I wouldn't die.

I went home after day four, again heading straight to bed. Staying upright was too daunting, but I tried to remind myself: *You are strong. You are brave. You can do hard things.* That night wasn't as rough. I still had vivid, weird dreams, but at least I was less restless and felt like I slept for a few hours at a time. I awoke the next morning with a sense of freedom and a physical lightness throughout my body. Was this what sobriety felt like? Had I made it over the hump like the counselor had promised. I was cautiously optimistic and took a hesitant step out of bed. I was pleasantly surprised when my steps felt stable—no spinning of the room—and the sunlight didn't cripple me. I was exhausted and stayed home from school again to rest, but when I arrived at my afternoon session, I felt like I was in control of myself. I listened to others share their struggles and experiences and realized I was not alone. I wasn't ready to share my story, but I gained strength and perspective by hearing theirs.

Before I left, the counselors introduced me to an app they recommended to help with sobriety. Why hadn't I thought of that before? I use apps for almost everything else; why should sobriety be any different? I wanted every possible strategy to help me be successful because the thought of going through the hell of withdrawal again was too much to bear. The counselors assured me that the app would reiterate many of the concepts we would cover in our upcoming meetings and had built-in resources to elaborate on topics of interest. I downloaded it immediately.

Day five of sobriety. I hadn't made it five days without alcohol in the last year. It was a major milestone, yet also devastating to realize that my drinking had rendered me so low. How did I get to this point? I had asked myself that question repeatedly over several months of therapy. Yet I knew it was okay to be proud. I needed to own it. I continued with the daily sessions and finished the initial two weeks that Dr. Prescott had signed me up for. I found myself wanting more, and I asked if I could continue attending the afternoon sessions on a drop-in basis. The counselor said I was always welcome, and Mom felt it was a good idea.

I didn't go every day but found myself sitting in the familiar chair about once a week. I started to open up in some of the sessions and felt like I was helping the newbies by sharing my experiences, just like others had done for me in my early days. Who would have thought I could be a role model? Having this outlet kept me accountable and also served as a warning against relapses whenever I witnessed others in the beginning throes of withdrawal. Watching withdrawal while I was sober was an eye opener and a harsh reminder of how dependent I once was on such a controlling substance. I tried desperately to sear the memory into my soul just in case I would ever become tempted by any sort of drug, legal or otherwise, to serve as a crutch again.

Thankfully, the program worked. I hadn't even been tempted to touch Mom's wine or had a desire to pick up a liquor bottle from the kitchen cupboard. What a relief. I had conquered this vice, at least in the short term, and knew it would have tremendous effects of furthering my progress with other therapy. Dr. Prescott thought this could become a cornerstone in my growth and development. I couldn't help being excited but leery at the same time. Growth could be painful, and I was nervous about what chapter would come next. It might be something I wasn't even cognizant of, but I hoped being sober would give me a better edge to handle whatever was next. Without alcohol consumption, I found my thoughts to be far clearer and more organized than they were before. My mornings were no longer characterized by a veil of dazed thoughts. Rather, I awoke ready to conquer the day within a few minutes rather than hours later.

With newfound energy and clarity, I turned to embracing my artistic talents. I explored the city with my camera and my sketchbook, and found myself getting lost in the beauty of nature. My projects took on deeper meaning, and I felt a stronger sense of pride in developing a story behind the picture through the lens or on the paper. I found an outlet, a reprieve, and importantly a healthy alternative to achieving a high. Being sober gave me a new way to view life and find intrinsic joy rather than relying on any external factors or influences that could be so transient and fickle. Ms. Clayton guided me in creating a portfolio of different types of art and introduced me to new techniques and artists to help expand my interests and navigate through various styles. A brand new world, bright with promise, was inviting me to participate. I found myself lost in galleries, both in person and online, finally feeling like I belonged somewhere.

OVERWHELMED

The photography presentation with Julia went remarkably well. As Julia explained our premise, I successfully stood in front of the class without wanting to dash out the door or feel like I needed a drink to steel my nerves. I didn't actually contribute to the oral presentation, but being able to maintain an upright position with all eyes on me as others critiqued our work was an accomplishment. I was riding high on this and eager to share Holly's pictures with Mom. I brought the special book for her home that afternoon and laid it out on the table in the living room. I went to the attic to help myself embody the spirit of Holly, which I hoped would inspire me to find the right words when Mom got home, as I knew it would be a difficult conversation to navigate and I didn't want to ruin it.

I heard Mom's car in the driveway and met her at the door. Before she was able to say anything, I grabbed her hand and led her to the living room. I showed her the book and told her about the project and started to tell her about the undeveloped film I found in the camera, my words all gushing out at once, jumbled together. I cut it short because she just stood there and stared, an eerie silence falling on the room. She didn't say anything, didn't move to pick up the pictures, didn't move at all, hardly blinking. I couldn't decipher her emotions and took this as an ominous sign. I quickly grabbed the book and moved it out of sight. This clearly had been a horrible misstep on my part. I took one last look at Mom just standing there like a statue and then dashed for the stairs. I rushed to my room and shoved the book in my desk drawer. How could I have made such a mistake? Had I ruined the bond that Mom and I had finally formed? Stupid, stupid, stupid. One of my most painful failures to date.

Mom didn't come to my room like I hoped she would. I was desperate to try and make amends with her and restore our newfound relationship from the prior tenuous, shaky relationship. I didn't see her that night at all, and she was gone the next day before I left my room. I had royally screwed up. Thankfully, I had an appointment with Dr. Prescott that day. I rushed into her office and blurted out the whole story within seconds of sitting down. It felt so good to get it off my chest, and now I wanted her to tell me how to fix it. I didn't want to go back to the way Mom and I used to be. I finally found a connection and was distraught to think that I had ruined it.

Dr. Prescott guided me through breathing exercises because I was so riled up that I was hyperventilating, and the room seemed to be fading away. By focusing on her voice and guided imagery, I was able to slow my breathing and feel myself gain control. I calmed down and settled back into my chair with a deep, cleansing breath. I heard a slight cough behind me and realized Mom was sitting there the whole time. I was in such a hurry that I didn't even notice her in the back corner chair when I arrived. My astonishment turned to fear and then to relief and finally to confusion. Sensing the uncomfortable heaviness in the air, Dr. Prescott quickly explained that Mom had called this morning and requested to attend my appointment today. I was shocked. She didn't mention it to me, but after last night's debacle, when would she have had the opportunity?

Mom must have filled Dr. Prescott in on my photography project because she started talking about how seeing the pictures from Holly's camera had given her quite a shock and caused her to regress into reliving the days right before she died. Of course! How could I have been so dense? All I had considered was how excited Mom would be to see these lost memories, never considering it might cause pain and anger instead.

"Marissa, it was such an impressive gesture to go through the struggles of getting the camera to work, retrieving and preserving those pictures," Mom said. "You could have no idea that they were in fact pictures that Holly took the day before she died when I visited her at college for a surprise lunch. They are the last memory I have of my sister."

Mom's revelation made her reaction more understandable. I realized that it wasn't about something I did wrong, but rather that it stirred conflicting emotions within her. She continued to talk about how she was so thankful to have physical evidence of those memories, as the ones in her mind were starting to fade. Going through the last few months of my depression and cry for help were making her face previous struggles that she had kept literally locked away. With Dr. Prescott's urging, I told Mom about how I explored the attic and found all the boxes of what I now know to be Holly's possessions. She started to cry softly and explained that she couldn't cope with the pain of her sister's death at the time, but felt so responsible for missing the signs that she couldn't part with her things either. Holding onto her belongings was instinctual yet had become a source of proof of her failure to help Holly.

Dr. Prescott suggested we start doing some therapy sessions together, explaining that Mom would likely benefit from individual therapy just like I had. This seemed like a good step forward, as we obviously were still struggling to communicate with each other, and various topics made us feel like we were walking on eggshells around each other. Understanding the other's viewpoint would help both of us move forward. We scheduled an appointment for the next opening that Dr. Prescott had available.

SHOCK

As I opened the door to leave the office, I almost ran into Annika, who was on her way in. She darted inside quickly with her head down. I was dumbfounded. I doubt she recognized me from school, since almost nobody ever did, but I certainly knew her. I had been spending so much time in the art wing that I wasn't in the know like I used to be, but suddenly memories of days past when gossip was the thing I thrived on came flooding back. Why would Annika be going to therapy? I felt the immediate need to know but realized just as quickly how tenuous my progress was that such a fleeting encounter could pull me back into my old habits.

The last rumor I remembered was Annika might be pregnant and not going to college. And I remembered at the dance after-party how she hooked up with Collin, was interested in cocaine, and had been starving herself to get into her dress. The more I recalled, the more I realized that the external picture-perfect life she portrayed to our peers was a sham. She probably struggled with the same need for approval that I did. Instead of idolizing her, I started to empathize with her. The act she must maintain was likely grueling and would be a daily battle. While her struggles were related to being in the limelight, juxtaposed to my struggles of never being seen, I couldn't help but feel a kinship with her.

The realization that other people struggled just as much as I did and hid it so well unnerved me. We hide our emotions from our family, friends, and outside world so instinctively as if we are afraid to show our human essence and uniqueness. How did we get here? Was it the pressure from social media and consumerism, or was it the very nature of being human that has existed for thousands of years? I was struck with a sense of relief that I was not so abnormal. Figuring out life was something everyone needed to come to grips with, and while mine was a bit more extreme of a journey, it was still a common problem for every single person. Oddly, I felt a small glimmer of comfort.

CONTEMPT

The day arrived for the joint therapy session with Mom, Dr. Prescott, and me. I was supposed to meet her there after school, as she was leaving work early to attend. I didn't know what to expect, and I went through the school day with anxious anticipation. Dr. Prescott asked that we come with an open mind, and she would lead us through the first session in a very guided fashion unless either of us had specific topics we wanted to address. I had a whole lot of things I wanted to address with Mom, but I was uncertain if I was ready to delve into it all.

We arrived at the same time on the sidewalk and exchanged an awkward smile. Mom broke the ice and said, "Well, let's do this. We're in it together." We walked into the room, and I sat in my usual chair with the structured back and firm, steady arm rests that I often braced myself with as I took deep breaths to reground myself. Mom sat across from me in the chair Dr. Prescott usually sat in, and I withheld my urge to ask her to move to the other chair. I wanted to keep things as controlled and predictable as possible. Beads of sweat were already dripping down my spine, and I could feel my shirt sticking to my back. Dr. Prescott quickly joined us to dissipate the deafening silence within the room. She made a few general statements about how this would stay a safe space and that we could openly discuss anything on our minds, though she would start a topic and see how it developed. We both nodded in agreement.

Topic one: "Are you spending time together at home?" We both nodded but didn't elaborate.

"When you are together, what types of things do you talk about?" Silence. I broke it first. "We talk about Holly sometimes."

"Good. Let's go with that. Why don't you tell me about the project with the pictures from Holly's camera again?"

Mom piped up. "Those pictures will forever be bittersweet memories, but I am so beyond thankful and blessed that Marissa retrieved them from the camera. Marissa, I don't think I ever said thank you. To relive those last days I had with Holly, not realizing they would be my last, allows me to see the light in her eyes and the laughter we shared that day. So many of my memories are locked away in those boxes of clothes in the attic. But they're mementos of the past and don't really embody who Holly was. The static nature of those things is so contradictory to her demeanor. She was a doer, always ready to take on the next adventure and trying to pull me along with her."

Here was my chance. I might not get another good segue. I blurted out, before I lost my nerve, "Mom. I need to confess to you how I found her camera. It has been weighing on me, and I need to tell you. It's true that I found it in the attic among her possessions, but the whole reason I went to the attic in the first place was to scope it out as a place to hang myself."

I immediately looked down in my lap, twirling my hair and fiddling with a string on my pants. I glanced up and saw the look I was afraid of—pure shock, pure terror, pure pity. I knew I had to get the rest out now or I likely would never address it again.

"I convinced myself the only way I would make others see me was to make a spectacle of myself by ending it all. I thought my death was the only way that people would ever know I had lived. My death would establish my existence. As I made my preparations, I found all of these different things in the attic, but I didn't know what they were. I sorted through them trying to glean some answers only to get discouraged, so I just pushed them aside to proceed with my intended plans. The only reason I am alive is because Julia rang the doorbell that day and interrupted my attempt. She saved me."

I let out a breath I didn't know I was holding. That was beyond hard, but I felt relieved. I looked up at Dr. Prescott first and then at Mom. Mom took my hand and squeezed gently. "I had suspicions you tried, but hearing you admit it is different. I feel like I failed you. Otherwise, how could you get so desperate and think your life didn't matter?"

I didn't want to hurt her, but I had to tell her. "Mom, you did fail me. All I ever wanted was attention—to be included in your life instead of being left at home while you went out and lived your life without me. Many of my deep-rooted issues are part of my never-ending struggle to be included. I blamed you for a lot of it, but I now realize you used it as an escape from dealing with your own issues. It doesn't make it okay, but I can at least start to understand it."

Mom immediately tried to defend her actions, telling me how hard she worked to make sure I had a good life, and I should appreciate the sacrifices she made. I felt myself closing down, building up a wall with tighter mortar than ever before. Dr. Prescott intervened quickly, feeling the original productive dialogue unraveling like a ball of yarn that a kitten had pushed down the stairs. She redirected us to the important fact that my attempt to kill myself had failed and I was still alive, sitting in this room and striving to overcome the shadows of depression. Neither of us was eager to return to a conversation. I certainly wasn't about to divulge any further thoughts at this point, and I slumped against the chair, feeling the rigid wood against my back. Mom also retreated and wouldn't make eye contact with either of us, pretending to look out the window despite the drapes being pulled closed. Dr. Prescott concluded the session with a reminder to take time to regroup tonight and make sure to talk to each other before going to bed.

Thank goodness we came to the session separately! I couldn't imagine riding in the same car with Mom right now. I absolutely needed some fresh air and some space. The session could have gone a million different (and better) ways, but ultimately I was glad that everything was out in the open. She needed to know, and I needed to stop hiding the secret.

RECONCILIATION

I was locked in my bathroom taking a bath when I heard Mom come home hours after our therapy session. Moments later, she knocked on the door. "Marissa, we need to talk."

Part of me wanted to scare her more, just to prove a point. I stayed silent, not allowing a sound from even the tiniest splash of water, and I staved off a sniffle. Make her consider the possibilities, I thought.

"Marissa. MariSSA. MARISSA. Open this door right now."

I cleared my throat. Enough to let her know I was alive, but not compromising enough to engage in conversation just yet. I heard her exhale on the other side of the door. I could feel her presence lingering. After all the times I wanted her attention, now I wanted nothing more than for her to give me space.

"I'm going to make a cup of tea and would like you to come downstairs when you get done with your bath."

I heard her footsteps recede from my room and go down the staircase. I pulled myself out of the cold water and dried off, wrapping myself in the comforting towel, knowing that the next conversation was going to be rough. I joined Mom in the living room, pulling a pillow and blanket across my lap, serving as a barrier between us.

"Thank you for coming out of your room and joining me. Today did not go as smoothly as either of us wanted, and we need to clear the air. I know what you revealed was difficult to share, and I am proud of you for having the courage to do so. I responded poorly and should have given you more of an opportunity to elaborate about your struggles."

"Mom, I wasn't trying to hurt your feelings today. I needed you to understand how much pain I have been in for years and how gaining your love and inclusion mattered so much to me. When I wrote my goodbye note before I was going to hang myself, it was three sentences. That's it. That's all I had to say to you before I died. You haven't seen me for me in a long time. I know it is different now, and we have made a lot of forward progress, but it is still a fresh wound."

She nodded in agreement. "I know, Marissa. At least, I do now. I never realized my actions had such a negative effect on you. I was just trying to survive my own trauma and cope in the way I knew how at the time."

We sat in silence, but a better silence than this afternoon. Like a silent agreement of putting today behind us. Both of us were breathing easier and with a better understanding of each other's thought processes. It was enough of a peace treaty to go to bed as Dr. Prescott requested, and we agreed to try and finish our conversations without getting so defensive in the future.

FOOLISH

Each week the mailman brought more flyers from surrounding colleges and universities. At first, I threw them promptly into the garbage as soon as they came without giving any a second glance. There was no way I could consider a college yet; it was too overwhelming. Just catching a peak at the smiling, glossy faces on the postcards was enough for me to start sweating and hyperventilating. How would I ever be able to leave my safe zone? I was doing well, but within the constructs of what I could control.

Then, during study hall, I was looking through a photography magazine that Ms. Clayton had given me that morning. There was an advertisement that caught my eye. It didn't feel fake or offer an unrealistic promise of an easier life. It was for the University of Georgia—Lamar Dodd School of Art. I went online to learn more about the program, and after just a few minutes of scrolling through the class offerings and students' featured art pieces, I was thoroughly impressed. For the first time, I felt something stirring within me to look for something more than I already had in life—a path full of promise being illuminated for me. This was what I had been searching for over the last few years—something that made me intrinsically happy. Maybe, just maybe I could consider college as an option.

When the school day was over, I hurried home, dug the recent college flyers out of the recycling bin, and looked up the schools online. I started a notebook, one page for each potential school, and took notes on the programs they offered, location, tuition cost, and any other pertinent information. Hours went by, and I was only interrupted by Mom coming home from work and stopping by my room to check on me. I looked up and excitedly told her I was going to college. She looked surprised but immediately smiled, put her hand on my shoulder. and said, "Well, of course you are, my dear, if that's what you want." With her stamp of approval, I dove back into my research, and rather than feel the usual anxiety of so many options and considerations, I was enthralled with the possibilities and the promise of a new future.

I burst into Dr. Prescott's office the next day for our appointment and gushed about my plans for college, talking incessantly about what I had worked on the night before. She let me spew all the details. Then I sat back in my chair, took a big, invigorating breath, and waited for her to tell me how proud she was of me, how I had made so much progress, and how I had things so well under control. Instead, she looked at me and said, "You are in the enchantment phase. This is going to be grueling work, and you have big steps still to complete to make yourself ready. Remember how easily you slipped into your old ways when you saw your classmate enter the office the other day? Also, considering your recent recovery from alcohol, we don't want a relapse."

Talk about bursting my bubble! I couldn't believe her! My cheerleader for the last several months was telling me I couldn't do it! I stormed out of her office without a word, furious at her!

I headed back home but stopped dead in my tracks about a block from my house. I was such a bitch. The way I reacted had just proved her point. I lost control within seconds and handed over any credibility that I was mature enough or had made enough progress in my therapy to consider college a wise idea.

I sulked the last block home, thinking about how fragile my mind was and how susceptible it was to the slightest disruption. When I got home, I emailed Dr Prescott right away with an apology. I asked to reschedule the appointment I had hastily left that day, and I also told her that I realized my reaction was proof I needed more work on myself before I was ready to leave home or pursue college. I added that I trusted her and was ready to do whatever was necessary to get better. It felt refreshing to send the email, like the first steps on a new path. It reflected an honest viewpoint of where I currently was in my therapy, laying out a clear direction with an end goal in mind. An organized plan always helped me keep calm within the chaos of my life and kept me from allowing the "what-if" train to take over my mind.

COMMITMENT

Action step one: Go on a college site visit. I had never been on a college campus before and had no clue what it would be like. In my head, I imagined it would be just like high school except on a much grander scale. More groups of students to ignore me, more square footage, more sneers, more rejection, and more opportunities to feel like a failure.

I caught myself. This type of mindset would ruin me, just like Dr. Prescott warned. I grabbed one of my therapy workbooks, working through a few pages and prompts. It began to work its magic, and I shifted into a more positive mindset. For the last exercise, I was supposed to list three goals I wanted to accomplish. Three goals, just three. I could only think of my immediate goal of attending college, but that seemed impossible at the moment, so instead I chose three things that would lead me to college—go on a college visit, pick which schools to apply to, and submit an application.

I didn't waste any time tackling my first goal—go on a college site visit. I decided to start with the local college, Miller-Motte College, so I could complete the visit in a single afternoon without inconveniencing Mom (or even letting her know about it, in case it was a huge fail). Also, without having to make a long drive, I wouldn't talk myself out of the visit before I even arrived. I was pretty sure that I didn't even want to attend that college, since it was a vocational and trade-skill training school and didn't have the art classes I was interested in, but I needed to start with a small step before venturing farther away. Enough practice would create predictability, and I could develop coping mechanisms to handle my anxiety for future visits that were more pertinent to my field of interest.

I lucked out. The following week, there was an optional tour hosted by the guidance counselors from school to go to Miller-Motte for an informal introduction to the campus and its programs. I signed up immediately but noted the other names on the list and cringed—Annika, Tyler, Kyle, Collin, and Madison. Just great. They were definitely using this as an opportunity to skip out on class. I was nervous that they could skew this experience for me and destroy my desire to go on any future college visits. I asked Julia to come with me and act as a buffer. She was worried about missing math class, where she was struggling and had fallen behind, but she reluctantly agreed. I told her I owed her big time and invited her to come over after school that day so that I could help her get caught up in her math homework and even quiz her. I loved math because the problems led to specific, exact answers, plus it came easily to me, and I could at least offer my help when she was so willing to help me.

DEFEAT

We arrived at the main building on campus and were greeted by a senior student who shared the details of the school. It felt like a museum tour at first as we walked through some buildings, navigated a few sidewalks, and listened to him drone on. You could tell he didn't care at all about his role in today's visit. Soon enough, we were encouraged to go off on our own and explore the campus, as long as we were back to the bus by 2:30. Julia and I eagerly separated ourselves from the rest of the group and went in the opposite direction. We walked into a classroom, thinking we could sit in on one of the lectures that was about to start—boy, was that a mistake. It was a small class, and just after the professor started, he paused, glared straight at me, and said, "You don't belong here. This is not your class. Get out."

I froze in place. The beads of sweat poured down my back, lights started to swirl in front of my eyes, and then flashes of color interrupted them like a kaleidoscope. I tasted bile in my throat and felt someone pulling on my arm. I blinked and saw Julia nudging me out of my seat. She helped me out the door just in time for me to throw up all over the grass. We moved to a bench under a tree and sat in silence. It was worse than I imagined. Every insecurity I had about not being able to make it at college, of losing out on a future I had only recently realized I wanted, was triggered by this man calling my bluff and striking at my core fear. "You don't belong here." How true and disheartening.

Julia tried her best to boost my spirits, but it was a lost cause. I was frozen to the bench and had no interest in seeing anything else. We sat there until it was time to leave. I was silent on the bus ride back to school and went straight home rather than finishing the school day. I messaged Dr. Prescott to tell her about the debacle today and how in our next session I would need strategies to help address the panic I had experienced based on the confrontation in classroom. If I was going to be in new surroundings, I would need to know how I could better abort a panic attack, as I was obviously still struggling with fear and anxiety despite everything we had been working on. My solace was I was able to recognize areas that required improvement, so I wouldn't be stuck on the merry-go-round of anxiety forever—at least I desperately prayed I would not.

Julia came over after school as planned for me to help with her math. She spread out her book on the dining room table, and I looked at the trigonometry assignment she was supposed to redo in preparation for a quiz on the material the next day. Thank goodness it was something I already knew well because my brain was about shot for the day. We worked through each of the problems, and she felt far more ready for tomorrow's quiz than when she arrived.

As Julia started packing up her bag, she asked what had

happened at the campus visit today. I glanced up at her but couldn't maintain eye contact, embarrassed and ashamed by what she had witnessed. I tried to shrug it off as the bus ride had made me queasy and the classroom was hot, and it got the best of me. I snuck a look up to see if she was buying any of this.

Instead, she sat back down at the table and said, "Marissa, I know you are struggling through hard stuff, and it's okay to have bad moments or an entire bad day, but don't lie to me. I can't be there for you if you don't trust me and if you are trying to pretend that you are okay when really you aren't. I won't know when you are putting up a fake front versus being truthful. Friends don't have to pretend with each other. You can tell me the worst of it all, and I will still be here, not to necessarily give you advice or tell you how it should make you feel, but to just be here for you and love you unconditionally. That is, if you let me."

I didn't know what to say. This was the connection I had strived for my entire life. To have an actual friend I could share life with and not have to worry about all the nuances of trying to fit in or that one misstep would put me into a worse hole than before. To be content with just being myself. The silence in the room echoed louder than a symphony, and she stood back up to leave.

"Wait," I said before she could head out the door. "I am not always good with expressing my thoughts or feelings, but I need you to know that you are important to me. You are the only friend I really have, and you have no idea how critical you are to my existence and happiness. I have been riding life solo since I can remember, and so it is hard for me to let someone else in. The day you first knocked on my house door with my artwork, I was about to hang myself in the attic. You literally saved my life. 'Thank you' will never be enough to express my gratitude for that day. Since then, you have shown up for me time and time again and proven that you are genuine. I need to be better at being a genuine friend to you."

Now it was Julia's turn to sit in silence with tears staining her cheeks. She reached for my hand, and I squeezed it back. I told her about how I had been in therapy with Dr. Prescott and on a much better path and that her friendship has been a cornerstone in my progress.

"We are more alike than I knew," Julia said. "I, myself had a close call with suicide a few years ago and understand all too well. This is not something you need to be ashamed of or try to hide from. My depression is something I still battle with, but I am on the winning side of it, and you will get there too. It just needs time and continued efforts."

My confession, and hers, gave me renewed faith in our connection and in the strength of our friendship, knowing there was no need to keep secrets. It was an unwritten rule established between us. Even on bad days, I could rely on her to understand and not have to pretend any longer. My breakdowns, flashbacks, and panic attacks would not make her run for the hills, and there was an amazing ease that came over me with that knowledge. Moreover, she would be uniquely prepared to help me through the worst of all those scenarios.

REFRESHED

Even with my failure at the initial campus visit, I knew I needed to do more of them to get used to different environments and interactions. Julia and I continued going on site visits together to explore possible school options. She was also interested in pursuing visual arts, and it gave us more time to hang out. We learned a lot about each other, including our favorite music, books, and foods. We eventually branched into philosophical discussions, which added so much depth to my previous shallow interests and reassured me that I was on the right path of growth and self-discovery. Each of the campus visits seemed to get a bit easier. At least the panic attacks had stopped, settling into a manageable level of nervousness and anxiety during my last two visits. I always needed a recovery period afterwards to decompress and process, but I made a lot of progress compared to that very first visit to Miller-Motte College.

After a few college site visits, however, I was no closer to knowing what school I might want to attend. I continued to use my trusty notebook and internet methods to try and narrow it down to a select few. I decided not to waste time on any further visits until I had zeroed in more precisely on a potential school. The deadline for submitting applications was approaching, and I didn't want to lose my chance for a fall enrollment, even though I was unsure how it could conceivably happen at this point. Thankfully, there was a universal application that could be submitted to several schools using the same forms and essay, so at least I didn't have to stress out about writing several essays for different schools. There were a few that required more of a portfolio submission, but only for those who were granted an interview for scholarship consideration.

Having procrastinated over the application process, I decided I needed to get started. I picked an evening after school, logged into the correct website, and settled in with popcorn and licorice. I filled in the easy demographic information on the first page of the application with no problem. The second page was more in-depth, asking for transcripts from the school and my scores from the standardized tests. Did I even take those? I tried to recall through the blur of my prior days. I faintly remembered sitting for a test in the library but didn't have the slightest idea if that was the ACT or not. I grabbed a Post-it Note to make a list of action items for tomorrow and decided this was enough progress for the day. Small steps lead to great things.

It turned out that I did, in fact, take the ACT that day in the library. How concerning that I took such an important test without being in the right state of mind! I had the office secretary help me find the log-in to obtain my scores and also put in a request for the transcripts I needed. I was too embarrassed to look up my results while I was in the office, fearing they would be abysmal since I didn't even recall taking the test.

Once I got home from school, I logged into the website immediately because if my scores were awful, I would need to arrange for a retake as soon as possible. I clicked the enter button, snapped my eyes shut, and whispered to myself that whatever it was, it would be okay. Just open my eyes and deal with it; I can't change the past and can only go forward—just a bunch of words to soothe myself before looking at what I thought would be inevitably bad news. I took a deep breath that I felt all the way down to my toes and opened my eyes to surprising news—a total composite score of a 27. What!?!?!? How did I pull that off? What a relief. One less thing to worry about, since my to-do list seemed to be getting longer and longer with each passing day as I moved closer to the end of high school.

I went back to the application website and entered in the newly acquired information of the composite ACT score and the individual components in addition to the code needed for the transcripts that the secretary gave me today. Section 2 was complete. Onto the next section—a list of high school activities, honors and achievements, community service, work history, family obligations, etc. Oh, this could be a problem. How was I supposed to account for the first few years of high school revolving around my gossip obsession, which left no time for club activities or participation? I would never get into college. I hardly did anything extra in high school outside of just surviving it.

DEDICATION

I initially skipped the section on school activities and achievements, but every time I opened the application, there was a literal red flag next to the section reminding me that it wasn't completed yet. It served as a condemnation that I had wasted my high school years. I ignored opportunities to participate in clubs and activities, despite hearing teachers say that "this would look good on a college application." I finished the section hastily so I wouldn't have to see it as a reminder of my failures at being a teenager every time I opened the application. I managed to include a few things—honor roll, the art award I received, a math competition I unknowingly participated in, the food drive I helped with during my freshman year. At least there wouldn't be an obvious big blank, empty section on my application.

I felt like I wanted to account for the countless hours of therapy, self-analysis, and work I had completed over the last several months. Did that fall into the family responsibilities category or the work category? My depression and suicide attempt certainly occupied much of my time for most of high school, and having the strength to prevail through it and set goals for the future was monumental. But how could I make my application reflect that? I didn't necessarily want to write my essay about it and come off like I was saying "poor me, pity me for my struggles and let me into your school." I also didn't want to sound self-righteous that I had made it out to the other side and should be rewarded for such. Either one seemed like a disingenuous ploy.

I decided to list it as work experience. Definitely a stretch, but it would get noticed and maybe lead to a discussion about it without me having to lay it out as an essay/self-reflection. I would need to work on my response when asked about it to make it concise and personal while staying confident and not getting derailed by anxiety. I listed it out as if it were a job—the employer as Dr. Prescott and the number of hours worked per week, including therapy sessions in addition to the self-directed workbooks and apps I had completed in my personal time. That came to a total of 10 to 15 hours per week. That felt reasonable, as if someone worked a normal job twice a week.

I felt accomplished in my progress on the application for the day. It was about half-done, as measured by the progress slidebar on the website. I looked ahead to the next section—letters of recommendation. That didn't seem too hard. The work was really on them, but who would I ask? Definitely Ms. Clayton—she was paramount to my recent interest in college and had pushed me to embrace my passion for the visual arts. I needed at least one more person. Would it be ethical or even appropriate to have Dr. Prescott provide one? I would ask at our session tomorrow.

I closed my laptop for the evening and headed downstairs, only to find Mom sitting on the couch in the dark without the TV or even music on. She was just sitting there silently—eerie really. I said her name without a response. I tapped her on the shoulder, and she screamed, throwing her arms up in the air, jumping from the couch, tripping over the ottoman in the process and landing on her butt. I laughed, and she started to scold me, but all I could do was laugh harder. I flipped on the light, and Mom looked down at herself and started to laugh with me. Such a delightful sound filled the living room as I tried to help her up and she pulled me to the floor, wrapping me up in a blanketed hug.

I wondered what had her so lost in her thoughts that she didn't hear me come down the steps or call her name, but she brushed it off as no big deal, disregarding my questions with a wave of her hand. I presumed it was about Holly, but never wanted to broach the subject first because it still was a source of pain and uncertainty that felt tenuous, like a silvery strand of a spider web, every time her name was spoken.

PEACE

Tomorrow was Saturday, and we were going on an adventure. Julia, Mom, and I would be heading to explore the University of South Carolina. This was it—the big one. It was by far the most extensive campus visit to date and my nerves had me tied up in so many knots that I couldn't sleep. I kept going over the details of our travel arrangements, the itinerary once we were on campus, the areas I wanted to see, and most importantly how I would handle myself if a panic attack occurred, especially since we were going to be so far away from home and my safe haven. I paced my bedroom, going over the steps of mental accountability, breathing exercises, and grounding techniques that I could employ as needed.

Mom knocked on my door, took in the scene, and decided a late-night cup of tea was needed. She returned to the room with the tea, and we settled on my bed together. We talked through what I was worried about, and just the act of verbalizing it helped soothe me. I relaxed a bit, and Mom told me about how she visited Holly a few times on campus, how she was in awe of her independence and confidence, and that she saw so much of her in me. She was concerned about how college had disrupted Holly so significantly and worried about the possible detrimental effects to me as well.

I rested my head against her shoulder. I felt her freeze for a moment, as this was new, but then she stroked my hair behind my ear and went on to tell me all the dreams she had for me and how proud she was of me for getting through the last year. These were all the affirmations I had yearned for, and I embraced them. I must have fallen asleep listening because the next thing I knew, my mom and I both woke up, startled to be in the same bed together and equally startled to hear knocking on the front door. I glanced at the clock. Julia was here already. All of my preparations, and I was the one to get us off-schedule. I rushed down and let Julia in, and then flew back up the stairs, getting ready faster than I ever had and then grabbing my bag and my laptop. Mom impressed me with how quickly she pulled herself together, relaxing her usual standards of perfection but somehow looking perfect nonetheless. I told her she looked beautiful and was happy she was going to be along on this big day.

We pulled out of the driveway, only fourteen minutes behind schedule. Not too bad; we would be okay. The plan would still work. I needed it to work. I needed to keep control.

The rest of the travel was uneventful, thank goodness. We stopped for lunch near the campus. The tour was supposed to start at 12:30, but I wanted to eat beforehand, thinking that the butterflies would be too much for me to keep food down once we arrived. I ate light and was quiet at lunch. Mom kept glancing between me and Julia, shifting in her seat, talking about the good time we had made on the drive and the weather. I could tell she was nervous about what might happen in the next few hours. Me too, Mom. Me too.

INSPIRED

———

Mom parked in the parking lot for campus visitors, and we were immediately engaged by the breathtaking landscaping and flowers outside of the main hall. I was enthralled as we approached the double wooden doors with brass hardware. The details of the carvings were gorgeous and precise, weathered slightly but astounding nonetheless. I had a good feeling about the day. We registered without problem and sat in the auditorium on the side aisle in case I needed to have an easy exit. The room soon filled with other eager students and family members, and the chatter reached almost deafening proportions, turning to a loud hum rather than individual voices. I felt a little swirl start in my head, but Mom handed me a cold bottled water just in time, and I was able to abort the feeling. The speaker started, the noise level immediately fell, and the first potential derailing was avoided.

We were split into small groups for the remainder of the tour, and I was incredibly thankful as it seemed far more manageable. We started with a leisurely walk through the beautiful grounds. Being outside was a saving grace. The other students in our group engaged in conversation with us, and I enjoyed the sense of inclusion. Maybe college would be different than high school. I could only hope. Then I began wondering. Was the fact that I was in a better mental place the reason that people wanted to initiate a conversation with me? Had my previous demeanor been the deterrent all along? Maybe the problem wasn't my peers; maybe it was me. Perhaps I was too isolated, too closed off, and too judgmental of everyone else that I was blind to the walls I erected that prevented the very objective I desired. Holy shit. Was I to blame all along? No, I tried to tell myself. That was part of it, but it couldn't be the whole story. It just couldn't be. I felt the color drain from my face, felt my footsteps getting slower and heavier, and had the desire to sink onto the nearest bench.

Julia grabbed my arm and directed my attention to the next building we were approaching, the arts and communications building. I snapped out of it. I shook my head slightly, blinked a few times, and focused. This would be the highlight of the whole day, and I wasn't about to let my crappy, anxiety-filled tailspin ruin this moment. I had worked too hard in therapy to allow defeat. I could further explore my own contributing role to my desolation with my peers on a different day.

Upon entrance to the building, our focus was drawn to the incredible displays of mixed media highlighted along the walls. The beauty of it left us all speechless. Mom was even impressed. Until now, she had believed art was more of a hobby than a realistic profession, but seeing the various ways that art could be used across platforms had her talking about it for the rest of the afternoon. She seemed to finally understand that I wasn't pursuing a pointless field of study but was making a formidable career choice. We made a few other stops to check out the dormitories and the library, and then returned to the main hall for a closing session that covered the application process, financial aid, and more administrative details.

Before leaving campus, we made one more sweep through the arts building. While Mom and Julia used the restroom, I sat in awe of one of the pieces before me. A student sat down next to me. She was talking on her phone at first but finished her call and then started chatting with me. She asked if I was headed to Dr. Olson's lecture next, and I informed her that I was just there for a campus visit and not enrolled. She gushed about the school and the classes she was taking and how I would not regret going there for even a second and then rushed off to her class before I could even get her name.

We headed back to the car for our drive home. I was so proud of myself for how I handled the day. I never dissolved into a panic attack, despite a few close calls. I managed to interact with a stranger and rather enjoyed the afternoon.

It was astounding to have a *normal* day when so often I had failed at the minimum of existing through previous days. I allowed Julia and my mom to carry the conversation on the way home, as one of the thoughts of the day resonated through me. Was my depression and anxiety the culprit of not fitting in through high school? The very goal I had strived for relentlessly and failed at was likely my own doing, even though it was at a subconscious level. I started berating myself and getting down on myself for wasting those years, but then I heard Mom's voice. "This could be the start of a whole new chapter for you, Marissa. You looked positively in your element on that campus today, and I saw your success lying there waiting for you to take it."

I slashed the negativity from my brain and focused on the here and now. I could not change the past and could only live in the present. Who cared about the whys, hows, or whats of the last few years? Those no longer mattered. Holding onto the past would only drag me backwards, and I only had intentions of moving forward and growing into the life that awaited me. I would not let the familiar grips of doubt coax me into the dark depths of despair that easily when I had a clear path toward stability. I could only control what was in front of me, and right now that was getting into college and pouring my efforts into not only finishing my degree but thriving. *You are strong, you are brave, and you can do hard things;* I repeated this over and over until I believed it.

REFLECTION

Personal essay. This was the section I feared the most, but now more than ever, I was convinced I could go to college, and this was the next action step to my plan. The natural topic to write about was my depression, my therapy, and my journey through it, but I really did not want to write about it here. It was too personal; it was too raw and too new. I didn't want people reading it and instantly getting a perception of who I was in seconds and think of me as another lost teenager who found her way. I appreciated the irony of me still fighting for someone else's approval. It's like a merry-go-round of issues, but this seemed different.

I spent the afternoon at the park, getting some sunshine and appreciating life's beauty around me, trying to gather inspiration as I sipped my coffee. Sitting in silence had become a luxury of mine. No distractions from my phone, no social media, no music, just the sounds of the world and nature that surrounded me. I often would get glares from people as they walked by, like I was a sociopath for just sitting there doing "nothing." How comedic, as they were truly the ones wasting their time with pointless scrolling, getting the perfect filtered picture, and trending rather than taking in the surrounding world.

Aha! That was it. My personal essay would be about how young people are losing their identity through the use of technology and social media, engaging in false perceptions so insidiously, so unintentionally that they become an adult without even knowing who they are. I could include my experience with depression and how it was linked to excess use of technology, not developing real friends, not having a grasp on reality since everything was perceived through a filter, and making harmful comparisons to people's lives as they want you to perceive them instead of how they actually are. I could touch on the relevance of this to my personal life without having to go into the deep details of my own depression and struggles.

This was an issue that affected my entire generation and was more prevalent than many were aware. I thought of Annika, Madison, and even Kyle and Tyler. The stars of the high school. But not really. As proven by Annika going into Dr. Prescott's office, she was struggling too. Every single peer I could think of was trying to figure out who they were but were getting lost in the shuffle as they compared Instagram feeds, Facebook profiles, and TikTok videos, while trying to one-up each other with more likes, more shares, and by becoming an influencer. People didn't realize real connections were being lost until it was too late, compromising their own sense of self along the way.

As I sat on the bench with this new premise in mind, I continued to observe those walking past, and I didn't see a single twosome who proved me wrong, whether it be friends or a couple. They were both on their phones as they walked, sometimes showing the other something on the screen, but mostly absorbed in their own little world, one app at a time, merely sharing space with each other without even connecting. How disheartening that the true human connection was right in front of them, yet they had the notion that true meaning to their life was within the virtual world.

No wonder the mental health of the collective American population had suffered so much. Every other article, news headline, or study seemed to be focused on the drastic increase of depression, need for self-care, and focus on bettering your mental health. The irony was that the harder someone worked at all the things listed within these recommendations, the more they depended upon technology and deepened the need for approval by someone else's standards instead of truly evaluating what they considered to be important and set their own guidelines.

Through the last several weeks I had learned more than ever before about how progress through counseling was supposed to look, and outside of the assignments that Dr. Prescott gave me with the linked apps and workbook, not one other app had proved beneficial. I had tried speed-tracking my progress and rise from depression only to face setbacks when I tried to take the promised quick-fix shortcuts. The nitty-gritty work was hard and grueling, but it was the only sure way to establish a new foundation that would be solid in years to come. Developing yourself from the ashes of a fiery depression was stronger than any future battle you might encounter; it was, at the very essence, required.

I hurried home to put pen to paper—metaphorically speaking—before my thoughts were lost in the whirlwind of my brain. I fervently typed out everything I could think of and would organize it later. The real challenge would be to pare it down to the word count required for submission.

DETERMINED

All right. Final review time of the application before submitting. I did it. It was complete. I went through each page and ensured the correct information was present. I re-read my personal essay. I double-checked the email addresses for my letters of recommendation. I analyzed the list of schools I was applying to, took one last big breath, and hit the submit button. That was it. No turning back now.

The application went off into cyberspace to my designated schools. To hedge my bets, I had included all the surrounding area universities and tech schools that had a visual arts program, hoping to get into at least a couple of them. I only wanted to go to maybe three of them on the whole list, but feelings of self-doubt stopped me from being too optimistic. I had convinced myself that getting accepted to any of the schools would count as a win. I still needed to finish my preparations for leaving my house, attending a new school with brand new surroundings, adjusting to a new campus and teachers, all while not falling apart into pieces. I wasn't sure I had it in me to put the puzzle back together again if that would happen. It had been a grueling stretch, and there was still a long way to go—speaking of which, I needed to get to my therapy session.

Today Dr. Prescott was role-playing being a professor in a classroom, going through mock scenarios that might cause me to have a panic attack. I answered her pretend question, and immediately she had a follow-up question that challenged my point of view and made me respond with a defense. I started twiddling with my fingers, looking around me, feeling the lights get hotter and the sweat start on my neck. I cleared my throat, closed my eyes for a brief second, imagined looking into the ocean, and then responded with my rebuttal. This was something we had been working on for a while, talking through strategies, implementing guided imagery to calm me, and recognizing scenarios that previously would have caused a meltdown. The more we did these, the easier they became as I could anticipate my body's reaction and employ the appropriate method. We both knew we couldn't prepare for every scenario I would encounter, but getting a handle on some of the basics seemed prudent. I wanted to include everything I could in my toolkit.

After our exercises, we settled in for a check-in. I unveiled some of my fears to Dr. Prescott about going through with college and leaving the safety net I had developed around me. Namely, what if I was a complete failure and couldn't manage to get through my classes without anxiety taking over, depression setting in, and me never wanting to leave my dorm room? What if I got so desperate that I restarted risky behavior to achieve that sense of lightness again? The what-if train was a nasty thing that kept me awake so many nights and drove my anxiety through the ceiling. Dr. Prescott merely looked back at me and said, "Yup, what if?"

We sat in silence for a short time, but she broke it first.

"What if you take the chance and succeed?

"What if you excel at your studies and land a lucrative job?

"What if you meet your future spouse?

"What if you have adventures that you will someday tell your kids about?

"What if you accept who you are and your place in the world?

"What if you never look back?

"What if?"

There were never immediate answers to the questions that plague us in the wee hours of the night, but without taking a chance on something, then I knew I was destined to fail. I would be living in the past and be dwelling in a place of depression and anxiety. While I was uncomfortable with the unknowing of what was to come, it was better than the alternative. I left her office with a tentative optimism, like pulling back the branch before entering the woods and taking a cautionary look before proceeding into unchartered territory. *You are strong, you are brave, and you can do hard things.*

HOPE

Time seemed to be moving at a tortoise pace as I awaited any response from my college applications. I would have settled for even a no. But there was nothing, not a peep. I overheard conversations at school of people getting acceptance letters or offers of scholarships, and I felt left out yet again. The need for approval echoed through my thoughts. I started experiencing self-doubt about my application, wondering if I had submitted something incorrectly. I incessantly checked my email, and I reread my confirmation submission email countless times. There was no indication that I had done something wrong. I just needed to be patient. I didn't have a backup plan if I wasn't going to college.

I sat sulking, eating ice cream, and binge-watching a random show on Netflix, when Mom came home from work one day. She took one look at me and knew it was a rough day. I hadn't had one in a while, but at least I was still out in our shared space and not locked in my room by myself, closed off from the outside world. She left me alone at first and then returned with her own spoon and plopped right next to me. We enjoyed the night like that and didn't even talk about the day. We ate dinner in front of the TV, laughing at the terrible jokes in the show and discussing the character's wardrobes.

After a while, Mom left to clean up the kitchen. I flipped off the TV after staring blindly at the screen and not even watching the last episode. I needed to go to bed and restart again in the morning. As I walked up the staircase, I happened to glance at the stack of mail Mom had brought in when she came home from work, and there it was—an envelope from Anderson University. Mom must not have seen it when she brought it in earlier. I ran back down the stairs, taking them two at a time and nearly falling down the last three, grasping the envelope and ripping it open. My first acceptance letter. I jumped up and down, let out a squeal, and even cried. The proof that I could do it. I was going to college. Mom ran to me from the kitchen after hearing the commotion and was astonished to see such a 180-degree change in my demeanor, not understanding until I threw the letter into her hands. She joined in on the celebration just as heartily, matching my excitement.

The next two weeks were filled with responses, some acceptances and some rejections, but responses nonetheless. I deployed my typical organizational strategies, starting my research anew on all the schools that had accepted me. I had a new purpose and wanted to make the best possible choice of school based on several factors of strength of program, distance from home, costs, campus environment, and the important "feel" the school gave me. If something didn't seem quite right, it went to the bottom of the pile. My mental health would depend upon my feeling at ease.

Julia was going through the same process and had also received several acceptance letters in the last few weeks. On Friday night, we watched an old movie from my mom's stash of favorites, *Under the Tuscan Sun,* and compared which schools we had heard back from. We both had ranked the top five schools we were considering, two of which were the same. We talked about how cool it would be to go to the same school and be roommates. It seemed so lighthearted and fun to discuss this shared vision of our future, but there were also a few seeds of doubt planted in my mind as well.

What if I regressed and my mental health issues became all-consuming again? What if being my roommate would be too much for Julia to handle and we couldn't be friends anymore? My self-confidence started to falter, and I wondered if I could really take the chance of ruining this friendship. Our friendship might, in fact, only survive if we didn't go to the same school, as horrible of a prospect that seemed in the moment.

CONTENT

After being accepted to several schools, I had my ranking of what I considered to be my top five, and with Ms. Clayton's help, I narrowed it down even further to what she thought would fit me best based on her experiences with some of the programs. I planned to pursue my passion for visual arts and the creative process. I wasn't exactly sure where it would lead me in terms of a career, but I felt a continual pull toward it and thought that nurturing these creative tendencies would lead me down the right path.

I consulted Mom, Julia, and Dr. Prescott as I debated the final choice of what school would be the best fit and ultimately chose the University of South Carolina's School of Art and Visual Design. This was the campus where Mom, Julia, and I went on our adventure together and where I realized I could succeed. Everything about that day had put me at ease. The school and campus felt like a natural extension of my safe zone, and I hoped I would be able to flourish in the environment. I was excited but petrified at the same time.

The history of Columbia with its towering historic architecture and rich culture would be a great inspiration for my prospective projects, and I looked forward to being in a supportive environment which valued the impact arts can have on a community. I also was looking forward to a fresh start away from home, but still close enough for some security. Everything I thought was important in my early high school years was such a distant memory. I caught myself wondering why I ever thought being part of the popular crowd was so crucial, yet I knew I could never allow myself to forget it as it would serve as an important warning to keep from returning to darker days.

Don't get me wrong. I was incredibly nervous about the possibility of experiencing a setback in my mental health after all the progress I had made, but Dr. Prescott's intensive exercises had prepped me for several possible triggering events, and she reassured me we could continue with virtual counseling. This was such a relief because I did not want to start over with a new psychiatrist and rebuild the relationship, honesty, and familiarity with someone else. Truthfully, I wouldn't be that far from home and could still hold sessions in her office when I came home to visit Mom. Stability in this area was crucial, and I would be a fool to think otherwise. Now, more than ever, I would need to embrace my therapy exercises to hold myself accountable to the stressors of college life and continue to embrace the self-growth and discovery I had worked on so diligently over the last several months.

The crucial final factor in my decision to attend University of South Carolina was Julia would be attending as well. Not that friends should be a driving consideration, but having a connection with someone familiar for such a big life change would make it a smoother transition. We were going to be roommates in the dorm, thank goodness, as I could not imagine what living with a stranger would do to my anxiety. We talked about my concerns that she might get sick of my mood swings and the possibility that I might slide back into old habits, but she reassured me she could handle the possible rocky road and importantly would be there to hold me accountable. I had to let go of my fears and trust it would work out. I made her insist we re-evaluate the roommate situation every couple of months to ensure it was still working and not a threat to our friendship. She teasingly agreed but reminded me she had old demons that would need to be kept in check too. We would act as each other's support system to stay in the good and out of the bad.

With the decision made, I found myself giddy with excitement. Julia and I opted to move into the dorms over the summer and take the opportunity to acclimate ourselves to the campus with a fraction of the students. That would give us time to explore and establish favorite places to eat and have coffee, where to study, where to relax, etc. High school was winding down, and we were busy going shopping for dorm room essentials, packing suitcases, and gathering art supplies so that we would be able to set up a small studio in our room. I kept waiting for the crash of my depression to come roaring its ugly head, but surprisingly I felt calm, steady, and reassured. Every step of the preparations reaffirmed my choices and importantly, I felt ready. I smiled to myself. *You are strong, you are brave, and you can do hard things.*

RUMINATE

I was sorting through my closet one afternoon, putting my clothes into "keep," "maybe," and "get rid of" piles. Mom entered the room and sat wordlessly on the edge of the bed. She looked lost in her thoughts, and as her silence persisted, I stopped what I was doing and called out her name, pulling her from the grips of her deep reflection. She appeared sad and uncertain, as if she were debating what she wanted to say. I blurted out that I couldn't take her just sitting and staring at me and that if "you're not going to say anything, just get out."

Immediately, I tried to retract my words as I truly did not mean to sound so harsh, but Mom was already rising from the bed and heading for the door. As she walked past me, I extended my hand to grasp her fingertips. She glanced back over her shoulder and sighed. "Mom," I said, "I'm sorry. I didn't mean it. Please stay." She hesitated but relented and settled back onto my bed. She was still quiet as she weighed her words, and I continued my wardrobe sorting. I wanted to get this done, throwing out anything that reminded me of my dark days, trying to create physical distance between any of these ties. Tensions eased, and we even wound up laughing as Mom shared anecdotes of her days with Holly before she left for college.

Aha. This was the true dilemma for Mom. Me leaving for college was forcing her to relive the memories she had of Holly going through the same experiences. From everything I had learned about Holly, she sounded like an amazing person, quirky and independent, ready to take on any challenge and reach for her dreams. With each story Mom shared, I could hear the yearning in her voice to have her sister back with her, and I felt guilty for ever questioning her motives for keeping her a secret. I didn't know how to reassure Mom that I wouldn't meet the same fate as Holly.

I sat next to her on the bed, taking her hands and leaning my head on her shoulder.

"Mom, the last few months have been indescribably difficult for both of us," I said. "The absolute darkness that overcame me nearly took me from this world and would have blindsided you a second time, just like what happened with Holly. Our souls cry out with a pain we cannot find the words for. But look at our progress, both individually and together. We would have never been able to have this conversation even six months ago. There is still work to be done, but there is hope. I have absolutely zero concerns at this moment that I would ever contemplate suicide again. Might some of my old vices return or moments of stress bring depression to the surface again? Probably. But my inner voice has matured and has created its own self-identity so that I no longer strive to meet other people's definitions of what it means to be happy or centered. I am grounded in my own truths."

I heard Mom's breath escape and felt her shoulder shrug next to me, some of her weight shifting heavier onto me.

"How did you become the adult?" she asked. "I am supposed to be giving the speech of reassurance and encouragement, and here you are boosting my spirits and calming my fears. Everything you said is true, but I do need to add that the most important part is that we are in this together. Neither one of us should ever feel isolated and alone. After everything that has happened in the last few months, there should be no qualms about calling for help if we need each other. We are family, and that is the most important thing."

After lots of hugs and a few tears, Mom and I finished sorting out the closet and ended the evening sitting on the back steps under the stars. Normalcy. How strange that it was always within reach, yet seemingly so far away.

PROUD

Graduation Day. The official close of my high school career. I went through the cursory ceremony, despite being ready to completely leave the school in the dust. I listened to the speeches with the faintest interest, but I did feel a sense of pride in being part of a day that I just as easily could not have been a part of it. A chill went down my spine as I thought of the alternate outcome and how close of a call it actually had been. Fate had intervened and given me another chance at life, and I would take full advantage of the opportunity.

Thinking back to my darkest days, I was unnerved to consider how much of a different person I was at the time.

I didn't even recognize myself then versus now. One of the class speakers quoted Peter Heller: "Life is tenacious if you give it one little bit of encouragement." I absorbed this quote deep into my soul. So much truth and such a personal statement that each individual could adapt to their personal needs. While the speaker used it to invoke the promise of moving on from high school, I recalled standing on the edge of a chair in the attic with a rope and a simple ringing of the doorbell being the saving grace that nudged me toward life. I needed just a little bit of encouragement that I mattered, and evidence proved life was tenacious indeed.

I walked across the stage, received my diploma, and stood with my class for the last time, ironically next to Annika. A large portion of my early high school days revolved around Annika and the popular crowd's every move, and yet I couldn't tell you any recent news about any of them. Monumentally, I didn't feel excluded with that lack of knowledge. I was content. Scratch that—I was happy.

Mom beamed in the pictures with me in my cap and gown and was elated to host a party, but I quickly pointed out to her we really didn't have many people to invite. I didn't want a group of acquaintances or family members that I only met a few times when I was young to be included in this. This was a big deal, but only those close knew how big a deal it truly was. I suggested we do just a simple dinner with Julia and her parents, Ms. Clayton, and Dr Prescott. She relented, but insisted she was going all out with a fancy five-course meal at the very least and I could pick out the dessert. Her excitement was palpable, and honestly it was encouraging to think our relationship had blossomed in such a short time into something so authentic.

Helping me with my own depression forced Mom to face some of her own demons. Her therapy was working wonders for her as well, allowing her to blossom with self-confidence. She was spending more time at home with me and putting less focus on materialistic things that had served as a substitute and cover for her pain. She started inviting her friends to the house rather than going out and had begun trying new hobbies, which I was thrilled about, because honestly, I was worried about how she was going to cope when I left for college.

Mom surpassed my expectations. The dinner was delightful and felt like the perfect way to wrap up the turmoil of the last year. Ms. Clayton lingered after dinner, and we sat and talked about the upcoming college year. She told me about some of the local places to check out while I was in Columbia. She encouraged me to keep in touch, even though high school was over, and gave me her personal email and cell phone. "Don't hesitate to reach out if you need help with anything," she said. I tried to convey my deep gratitude to her but fumbled over my words. We parted with a hug, and she encouraged me to keep her updated with my projects and said that she was excited to see what I would create.

I sat outside after everyone left. Mom found me gazing into the darkness of the night. I loved the beauty of the stars, the stillness of the sky, and the smell of summer and new beginnings in the air. Many nights, I had gazed at this very sky and wondered if life was worth living, and now I could resoundingly say, yes it was. I may be a very small piece of the world, but I was placed here intentionally in this moment, and I would not spoil it or insult God by not fulfilling my purpose. My determination built with each day, and I finally felt confident I was on the winning side of my war with depression.

RENEWAL

The sunlight broke through the curtains, bouncing off the desk and shining on the stack of totes by the door. Today was the day. I was going to college. I had made it. The hallmark event that confirmed I had survived high school. The precipice of a new adventure. I reflected on the last four years, and sadness crept over me for a split second before I changed focus to the upcoming move, settling into my new dorm room, exploring the campus, pursuing my passions, and declaring a new chapter in life.

I was lost in my own thoughts, resisting the urge to jump out of bed and begin this new adventure the moment the sun snuck through the curtains. I must have lost track of time, though, because I heard the incessant doorbell ringing once again and smiled to myself, knowing it was Julia, ready to embark on our next journey together.

You are strong. You are brave. You can do hard things.

RESOURCES

While this is a fictional story, it is based on very real issues plaguing our youth. If this book struck a chord with you and you found yourself saying, "me too" or "that's me," please use it as an opportunity for a conversation-starter. Have your loved ones read it, and then discuss it together. Have the courage to reach out to a counselor or psychiatrist, or take solace in knowing that you are not alone. Importantly, use the resources listed below as needed if you find yourself in desperate scenarios.

National Suicide Hotline: 1-800-273-8255

Crisis Text Line: Text **"HOME"** to 741741 from anywhere in the United States, anytime. A live, trained crisis counselor receives the text and responds from a secure online platform. The volunteer crisis counselor will help you move from a hot moment to a cool moment. This is available 24/7 and is a free service.

YouthLine: text **"teen2teen" to 839863, or call 1-877-968-8491.** YouthLine provides a safe space for children and adults ages 11 to 21, to talk through any issues they may be facing, including eating disorders, relationship or family concerns, bullying, sexual identity, depression, self-harm, anxiety, and thoughts of suicide. This is available 24/7 and is a free service.

SAMHSA National Helpline: 1-800-662-4357. The Substance Abuse and Mental Health Services Administration is a resource that is confidential, free, 24-hour-a-day, 365-day-a-year and is for individuals and family members facing mental and/or substance use disorders. This service provides referrals to local treatment facilities, support groups, and community-based organizations. Callers can also order free publications and other information.

ACKNOWLEDGMENTS

To Little Creek Press and staff: for your expertise and special touch on this project and making my bucket list item of writing a book turn into a finished product. Specifically, to my editor, who turned my novice writing into a polished piece for ease of reading. I will forever be grateful to all of your wisdom and guidance throughout the process.

To my husband: for always being supportive of my dreams, no matter how wild they may seem. Your love and stability allows me to stretch and take forward action on making my dreams a reality. Thank you for tolerating "just one more" opinion on an array of aspects that made this book complete. I love you.

To my children: for being a driving force to chase my dreams. Showing you by example that it's important to have big dreams and pushing to achieve them. Thank you for being so proud of your mama and telling everyone, "my mom wrote a book!!" I love you.

To my parents: for creating an environment while I was young in which books were not only normal, but exciting. Trips to the library, ordering from the monthly book orders and the book fairs at school were always a highlight of my childhood. Embracing literacy from a young age certainly has made a lasting impact on my life. Thank you, I love you.

To my dearest friend Cassie: I am not sure if this book would've ever finished without you. The countless hours on your couch of either fast keystrokes of diligent work, or my sounding board when I questioned if anyone would want to read my book, to being one of the first to read the first rough draft. Your continued friendship makes me hear criticism as well as encouragement, thank you.

To all of my English teachers throughout life: for encouraging a love of the written word and opening a new world to me at an impressionable age. Being part of my first book club in seventh and eighth grade, thanks to a couple of amazing teachers, made me realize and embrace that reading was allowed to be a hobby. Since then, reading has been a constant source of relaxation, rejuvenation and reprieve.

ABOUT THE AUTHOR

Laura Schultz is a Wisconsin native, raised in a rural community where she continues to reside with her husband and two children. She earned her Master's degree in Physician Assistant Studies at Marquette University and continues as a practicing PA, spending the last twelve years in emergency medicine. Her time spent treating patients struggling with mental health served as inspiration for her debut novel, *kNOT unDONE*. Becoming an author is a dream fulfilled and opens the doors to a world of new chapters.

To contact Laura: authorlauraschultz@gmail.com
@authorlauraschultz

Made in the USA
Monee, IL
11 April 2022